GW00983356

EDINBURGH

Compact Guide: Edinburgh is the ultimate quick-reference guide to this historic destination. It tells you all you need to know about the attractions of Scotland's capital, from the city's famous castle and Georgian architecture to its great art galleries and cutting-edge festival.

This is one of 133 Compact Guides produced by the editors of Insight Guides, whose books have set the standard for visual travel guides since 1970. Packed with information, arranged in easy-to-follow routes, and lavishly illustrated with photographs, this book not only steers you round Edinburgh but also gives you fascinating insights into local life.

Part of the Langenscheidt Publishing Group

Insight Compact Guide: Edinburgh

Written by: Roddy Martine
Updated by: Stephen Khan
Photography by: Bill Wassman
Additional photography by: Pete Bennett 6, 7, 23, 25, 26, 27/1, 37, 38, 39/1, 39/2, 40/1, 41, 43/1, 51/1, 64, 70, 75/2, 83, 84, 96; Berlitz 13; Douglas Corrance 21/2, 47/2, 52/2, 65/1, 71/2, 74, 84, 97, 98, 103, 116; The Fringe 102/1
Cover picture by: Doug Pearson/Jon Arnold Images
Picture Editor: Hilary Genin
Maps: Apa Publications

Editorial Director: Brian Bell
Managing Editor: Maria Lord

CONTACTING THE EDITORS: As every effort is made to provide accurate information in this publication, we would appreciate it if readers would call our attention to any errors and omissions by contacting:
Apa Publications, PO Box 7910, London SE1 1WE, England.
Fax: (44 20) 7403 0290
e-mail: insight@apaguide.co.uk

Information has been obtained from sources believed to be reliable, but its accuracy and completeness, and the opinions based thereon, are not guaranteed.

Worldwide distribution enquiries:
APA Publications GmbH & Co. Verlag KG (Singapore Branch)
38 Joo Koon Road, Singapore 628990
Tel: (65) 6865-1600, fax: (65) 6861-6438

Distributed in the UK & Ireland by:
GeoCenter International Ltd
Meridian House, Churchill Way West
Basingstoke, Hants RG21 6YR
Fax: (44) 1256 817988

Distributed in the United States by:
Langenscheidt Publishers, Inc.
36-36 33rd Street 4th Floor
Long Island City, New York 11106

www.insightguides.com

Introduction

Places

Culture

Travel Tips

◁ **National Portrait Gallery (p55)** Built in the 1880s in flamboyant Gothic style, this museum contains many portraits of celebrated Scots, including Robert Burns, Robert Louis Stevenson and Mary Queen of Scots.

▽ **National Gallery of Scotland (p49)** One of the best art collections in Europe, from Old Masters such as Raphael and Titian to Monet and Cézanne.

△ **National Gallery of Modern Art (p62)** The great names of the 20th century — among others, Picasso, Matisse and Giacometti — along with fine works of Scottish art.

△ **Royal Botanic Garden (p63)** A world-famous garden, with many exotic plants, which dates back to 1670.

◁ **Charlotte Square (p51)** Designed in 1791 this is considered to be the finest square in the city.

△ **Edinburgh Castle (p24)** Edinburgh is defined by its castle and its festival, and every August the two combine at the Military Tattoo.

◁ **Calton Hill (p44)** This volcanic outcrop crowned with monuments, has panoramic views of the city, Holyrood Palace and the Firth of Forth.

△ **Museum of Scotland (p39)** An outstanding new museum, built in 1998, recounting Scotland's history.

▽ **High Kirk of St Giles (p28)** The cathedral of the Church of Scotland.

▷ **The Festival (p104)** The world descends on Edinburgh in August to take part in the renowned festival, a vast celebration of the arts. Many comedians have used the fringe festival as a launching pad to success.

A City Without Equal

Edinburgh is a city "that no place in the world can pretend to equal", declared Thomas Jefferson, the third president of the United States. A bold statement indeed, but walk down Princess Street on an August evening and you might be inclined to agree. It is a cultural malestrom unlike anything else on earth. New books, comedy, plays and music are showcased. Great minds discuss the issues of the day. As fireworks reach into the sky from the ramparts of the castle there is an energy and excitement about Edinburgh that few cities can match. But there is much more to Edinburgh than its summer festivals. For this is the capital of an ancient nation that's infleunce resonates around the globe. It has a proud indigenous history of artistic excellence, intellectual endevour and scientific discovery that is reflected in its new-found confidence and buoyant economy.

But while this is a city of great beauty, scratch the surface and you will find something of a dark side. Edinburgh's past is replete with tales of witchcraft, warfare, ghosts and death. Robert Louis Stevenson, a native, based *Dr Jekyll and Mr Hyde* on a notorious local murderer, and many have extended this parable of the divided mind to the city itself, contrasting its Calvinistic gentility with its low-life drug scene. The thin veil of middle-class respectability was famously torn off again in the 1990s by Irvine Welsh's novel *Trainspotting*, which was turned into an enormously successful film starring Ewan McGregor. Ultimately though, *Trainspotting* merely enhanced Edinburgh and Scotland's reputation as a hub of creativity.

ARCHITECTURAL EXCELLENCE

Thomas Jefferson's enthusiasm for Edinburgh referred specifically to the New Town, completed between 1767 and 1830 and the largest Georgian area ever conceived. It was planned as a model for urban living and in just one square mile (2.5 sq km) are 10,000 buildings listed for their architectural merit. Many are

Scottish smog
A century ago the city was known as Auld Reekie (Old Smokey) as a result of the noxious pall created by peat and coal smoke from the many chimneys in the Royal Mile and surroundings.

Opposite: tenements and shops along West Bow
Below: piper busking next to the statue of David Hume on the Royal Mile

still in private residential use. Edinburgh also has a remarkable medieval town, which sprang up around and along the spine of rock topped by the castle. In 1513 the Flodden Wall was thrown up to defend the city from the English. Walls gave protection, but they also forced the people to live cheek by jowl in a complex of vertical tenements. Their legacy, though, is a unique and stunning city centre that has been granted UN World Heritage Site Status.

LOCATION AND SIZE

Strategically situated inland from the southern shore of the Firth of Forth, an estuary of the North Sea on Scotland's east coast, the capital has spread in every direction. Like Rome, the city is built on seven hills. Rising above Princes Street, the main shopping promenade, is the castle rock, a volcanic plug where the first defensive settlement was founded over 2,000 years ago, and a landmark to anyone who is lost. To the south is the Old Town, sloping east along the Royal Mile, beyond the Flodden Wall and towards the parkland of Holyrood. To the north, between the castle and the Port of Leith on the Firth of Forth, sprawls the New Town.

View from Calton Hill to the Palace of Holyrood

Edinburgh has just under 500,000 inhabitants,

but that number trebles in summer as visitors pour in for the festivals that help to make the city Britain's most popular destination after London. With the University of Edinburgh established in 1583, Edinburgh College of Art in 1909, Napier Technical College in 1964 (now Napier University) and Heriot-Watt University in 1966, there has always been a large student population.

THE CLIMATE

The weather on Scotland's east coast is drier and colder than on the west, but Edinburgh is notorious for the seasonal North Sea 'haar', a mist which periodically settles over the city like a grey blanket. When it does rain, a strong wind sometimes renders umbrellas useless.

Generally, however, summers are moderately warm, although often cloudy, and winters are cold but clear, with occasional light snowfall. For most of the year the climate makes for more of an indoor, than outdoor, existence, and locals, for the most part, tend to go about their everyday lives immune to the weather. When the sun does come out, however, the city is transformed, somewhat absurdly, with tourist and office worker alike taking full advantage of the many green spaces for sunbathing.

THE PEOPLE

The citizens of Edinburgh have a reputation for being reserved and somewhat prim. There's a saying that while 'breeding' in Glasgow, Scotland's competing city on the west coast, is thought of as good fun, 'breeding' in Edinburgh is considered good form. A variant is the Glaswegian accusation that Edinburgh women are 'all fur coats and nae drawers [*no underwear*]'. These jibes don't so much indicate any objective truth as underline the two cities' lasting rivalry.

The Edinburgh view is that the jealousy grew out of the city's 19th-century boom in middle-class clerical jobs in banking and insurance, which contrasted with Glasgow's reliance on

CLIMATE CHART

Edinburgh

☐ Maximum temperature
■ Minimum temperature
— Rainfall
✳ Sunny months

Sharing a stair
Edinburgh is unlike most British cities in having both a heavily residential city centre and a mix of classes, including an unusually high proportion of the middle class, living in the Victorian and Edwardian tenements of the inner suburbs. A desire for privacy within close confines and the near juxtaposition of social classes doubtless contribute to certain a reserve among neighbours when they pass on the street or on the common staircase, although beneath is usually a generous personality.

heavy industry. But it may date from the people's ingrained restraint, sprung to some extent from the Protestant religion in the 17th century.

CELTS AND PICTS

Below: the History of the Church of Scotland on display at John Knox's House
Bottom: James VI of Scotland who became James I of England

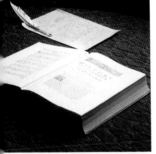

Whereas Glaswegians reflect their vibrant Irish/Celtic west-coast origin, Edinburgh evolved long before from Pictish, Saxon and Norman influences. The original Scots, a Celtic people from Ireland, had arrived on the islands and mainland of the west coast to form their separate kingdom of Dalriada. From the 6th century until Kenneth I, the 36th King of Dalriada, merged the two kingdoms, they systematically overwhelmed and integrated with the resident Pict community. In the 11th century, Saxons, fleeing from William the Conqueror, who had subjugated England, began to arrive on the border, and in 1124 David I (raised at the court of his brother-in-law Henry I of England) invited many of his Norman friends to accompany him when he returned to Scotland to become king. At the same time the people were subjected to Viking invasions and and an influx of other settlers from the north.

SCOTTISH CAPITAL

By the beginning of the 16th century, Edinburgh was established as Scotland's capital, and a professional class was spawned. A harsh blow to the people's self-esteem was dealt in 1707 by the Act of Union, which united Scotland with England under one monarch and parliament – based 400 miles away in London. Scotland retained its own Church and legislature, but the feeling that Edinburgh had become a hollow capital persisted until the end of the 20th century, when a Scottish parliament was elected.

THE SCOTTISH ENLIGHTENMENT

Political power ebbed from Edinburgh following the Act of Union, but intellectual influence did not. Towards the end of the 18th century, well into the 1800s and over a period which became known as the Scottish Enlightenment, the city drew together some of the most stimulating minds in Europe. In a tavern off the Royal Mile, David Hume, who wrote a six-volume history of England, would hold court with the physician William Cullen, the chemist Joseph Black, the mathematician John Playfair, the dramatist John Home, the first sociologist Adam Ferguson, and the first capitalist economist Adam Smith. For an all-too brief moment, the poet Robert Burns flirted with the Edinburgh salons of 'Clarinda', his sponsor, the wealthy Mrs MacLehose, and towards the end of this golden age Sir Walter Scott's novels had become best-sellers throughout Europe. Painters of the calibre of Henry Raeburn, Allan Ramsay, Jr, and David Wilkie documented the age, while the Adam family dazzled the nation with architectural achievement. It was Edinburgh's finest hour.

The city derives much of its character from that era of grace and elegance, although austere Calvinist doctrines encouraged a tension to develop between professional and artistic pursuits. But enjoyment is not always chained to restraint. There are now plenty of nightclubs which get custom from the large student population, and during the Edinburgh Festival in August, the city is the liveliest in the UK.

Aids capital

The city's prim image was decisively shattered when, in the late 1980s, Edinburgh was dubbed the Aids capital of Europe. The high per capita incidence of HIV owed less to sexual practices than to the sociable habit of needle-sharing among drug users, although the provision of clean needles did much to control the spread of the epidemic. The city's reputation for drug abuse has proved hard to live down, however, particularly given the popularity of such cult films as *Trainspotting*.

The elegant Ann Street in Stockbridge

THE GOVERNMENT

The first elections to a Scottish parliament in nearly 300 years were held on 6 May 1999, after a referendum had confirmed the people's wish to self-govern. This reflected a shift in Scottish public opinion since 1979, when the home rule option was rejected due to the 'yes' vote gaining less than a third of the whole electorate. Surveys have revealed that most Scots now consider themselves Scottish first and foremost, and British as an afterthought. The Parliament and Scottish Executive are based in Edinburgh, responsible for legislation and government in domestic matters, while Scottish constituencies continue to be represented in the separate British parliament, as part of the United Kingdom. Local government is run by the elected City of Edinburgh Council.

Below: Scottish National Party Headquarters, plaque detail
Bottom: Forth Bridge

THE ECONOMY

Edinburgh is a financial centre of international standing, founded on traditional virtues of prudence and propriety, combined with a flair for innovation. Furthermore, the financial services sector embraces banking, insurance and pensions, and Scotland now ranks fourth in the European Union for specialist fund management. This eminence shouldn't surprise: it was a Scotsman, after all (William Paterson), who founded the Bank of England in 1694. And it was Adam Smith, born in Kirkcaldy, a small fishing village near Edinburgh, who produced the 1776 masterwork *The Wealth of Nations*, championing the paradox of private gain yielding public good.

Edinburgh lawyers and accountants took Smith's doctrines seriously. In the late 19th century, they gathered together the surplus funds of Scottish industrialists and made fortunes by investing in such projects as American railroads and the rebuilding of Chicago after the 1871 fire.

For most of the 20th century, Edinburgh's financial institutions largely occupied the spacious rooms of the New Town streets between Charlotte Square and St Andrew Square, but new technology influenced an exodus to purpose-built accommodation elsewhere: the West End, where the Edinburgh International Conference Centre is located, is now known as the financial district, while some in the sector have moved to the Gyle Business Park, west of the city centre. In consequence, a number of the fine Georgian buildings in the centre are now being restored to their former residential glory.

TOURISM AND LEISURE

Tourism is important to the city's economy, while the Scottish parliament has brought a boom in business and the property sector. Sizeable office, retail and leisure developments have been springing up all over the city since the late 1990s, from hotels and offices on Holyrood Road to the 444,000 sq-ft (41,250 sq-metre) shopping centre, Ocean Terminal, at Leith.

THE LAW

Scottish Law remained, after 1707, distinct from English Law, and this variance, guaranteed by the Act of Union, has made an important contribution towards preserving a Scottish identity. Because Scotland broadly follows the Roman Law tradition, Scots tend to be much more in sympathy with European Law than are the English, who follow the English Common Law system.

Giddy aroma
Two traditional industries which survive in Edinburgh are brewing and whisky distilling. On balmy summer evenings the smell of malt wafts across the city from the Caledonian Brewery on Slateford Road and the North British Distillery at Gorgie.

Fireworks celebrating the end of the Edinburgh Festival

HISTORICAL HIGHLIGHTS

900BC Bronze Age settlement on what is now Castle Rock.

208BC–12AD Roman fortifications are built at Cramond.

600 Dun Edein, the fort on the rock, is occupied by Gododdin tribe before falling to Northumbrian Angles in 638.

843 Kenneth MacAlpin unites the kingdoms of Scots and Picts.

1125 David I makes Edinburgh a Royal Burgh.

1128 Holyrood Abbey founded.

1251 Queen Margaret, wife of Malcolm III is canonised by the pope 58 years after her death.

1286 Alexander III, the last Celtic King of Scots, is killed in a riding accident. The throne passes to his three-year-old granddaughter, Princess Margaret of Norway.

1290 Margaret dies on a ship off the Orkney Islands during her journey to Scotland to be crowned Queen.

1292 John Balliol, a distant relative to the Royal House of Scotland, is crowned King of Scots at Scone.

1295 Balliol signs treaty with France.

1296 Edinburgh Castle is captured by Edward I of England. Balliol is forced to abdicate.

1297–1304 First War of Independence. Led by William Wallace, the Scots rise up against the English. Wallace is captured and executed and the Scots defeated.

1306–28 Second War of Independence. Robert the Bruce successfully renews the struggle against the English. Treaty of Edinburgh recognising Scotland's independence is signed between Robert I of Scotland and Edward III of England.

1513 Flodden Wall is put up around the city after the Scots are defeated at the Battle of Flodden.

1544 Determined that the infant Mary Queen of Scots should marry his son, Henry VIII sends the Earl of Hertford to sack Edinburgh Castle (The Rough Wooing). Mary is sent to France for safety, and is betrothed to the Dauphin.

1559 John Knox is appointed Minister of St Giles' Kirk. Mary de Guise, mother of Mary Queen of Scots, as Regent of Scotland, defends Leith against the Protestant Lords of Congregation, who object to her Catholic politics.

1560 Treaty of Edinburgh, also called Treaty of Leith, is signed between the French and English recognising the sovereignty of Mary and her husband François II of France over Scotland.

1561 Mary Queen of Scots returns to Scotland when her husband dies. She astutely gives her official blessing to the Reformed Church of Scotland.

1565 Mary Queen of Scots marries her cousin, Lord Darnley.

1567 Lord Darnley is blown up in a house at Kirk O' Field, beside the Palace of Holyroodhouse. Three months later Mary marries the Earl of Bothwell.

1568 Mary Queen of Scots loses Battle of Langside against her own nobles and flees to England.

1571–73 Edinburgh Castle besieged by the Earl of Moray, in order to suppress the supporters of Mary Queen of Scots.

1582 Edinburgh University, the first to be non-ecclesiastical in Britain, is opened.

1603 On the death of Elizabeth I, James VI of Scotland becomes James I of England and Scotland.

1638 The National Covenant, objecting to the imposition of English Episcopalianism over Scottish Presbyterianism, is signed at Greyfriars.

1643 Solemn League and Covenant agreed between English parliament and Presbyterian Scots.

1645 The plague ravages Edinburgh.

1650 Charles II, having agreed to terms of the Covenant, is crowned at Scone. The Palace of Holyroodhouse is occupied by Cromwell's troops.

1660 Restoration of the monarchy in England and the sovereign in Scotland.

1695 Bank of Scotland is founded in Edinburgh.

1706 In an insurrection in protest against the proposed Act of Union, the residence of the Lord Provost is attacked and the army has to take control of the city.

1707 Act of Union passed. Government moves from Edinburgh to London.

1722 Last witch burned on Castlehill.

1736 John Porteus, Captain of the Town Guard, orders his men to fire on the riot at a public execution. He is condemned to death, then reprieved. The people break into the Tolbooth jail, and hang Porteus on a dyer's pole in Grassmarket.

1745 Prince Charles Edward Stuart arrives in Edinburgh with his Highland army, to win back the British throne for his father. He wins the Battle of Prestonpans and marches into England.

1767 James Craig wins competition to build the New Town of Edinburgh.

1786 Robert Burns visits Edinburgh, where he receives a rapturous welcome.

1822 Sir Walter Scott organises a levee at Holyrood Palace for George IV. The Honours of Scotland, the Sword of State, Crown and Sceptre, bricked up within the castle since 1707, are put on show.

1842 Edinburgh is linked to the UK railway at Waverley and Haymarket.

1844 The Scott Monument is erected.

1890 The Forth Bridge opens, providing a direct link with northeastern Scotland.

1947 First Edinburgh International Festival takes place.

1979 Referendum on the re-establishment of a Scottish parliament in Edinburgh is rejected.

1996 Stone of Destiny transferred from Westminster Abbey to Edinburgh Castle.

1997 Referendum votes in favour of a 129-member Scottish Parliament with tax-varying powers. Scientists at the Roslin Institute create Dolly the sheep, the world's first clone of an adult mammal.

1999 A Scottish Parliament is elected.

2004 The new Scottish Parliament building opens.

2007 Alex Salmond (SNP) is elected First Minister.

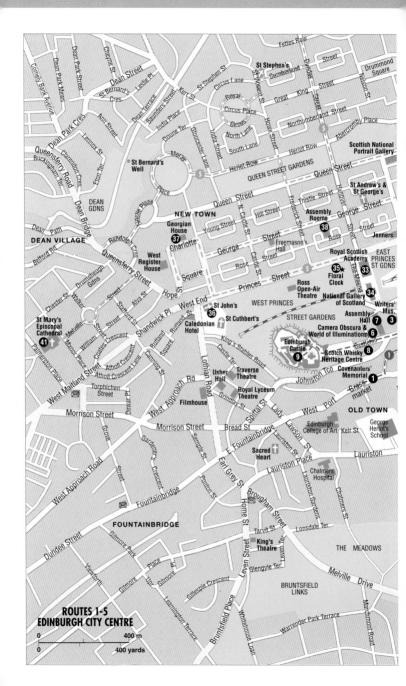

ROUTES 1-5
EDINBURGH CITY CENTRE

0 ———————— 400 m
0 ———————— 400 yards

Map
on pages
18–19

Map on pages 18–19

West Bow wizard

Victoria Street replaced the upper West Bow, which had zig-zagged steeply up to the Lawnmarket, causing consternation to those trying to haul goods to market. It is said to be haunted by a galloping headless charger ridden by a 17th-century resident, Major Weir, the 'Wizard of the West Bow' who was executed after confessing to a string of depravities.

Preceding pages: Royal Mile store selling tartans
Below: Covenanters' Memorial

1: Old Town and Castle

The Grassmarket – George IV Bridge – Gladstone's Land – Camera Obscura – Edinburgh Castle

The first route begins at the entrance of the old city and takes in the top of the medieval Royal Mile. It ends with a tour of Edinburgh Castle, including a visit to St Margaret's Chapel, the city's oldest building.

THE GRASSMARKET

★★ **The Grassmarket**, lurking below the south-facing drop of the castle rock, houses hotels and great pubs and restaurants, but long ago the monks of the Greyfriars held cattle sales here. At the east end is one of the old wells sunk to supply Edinburgh with its first clean water in the late 17th century. Beside it stood the public gallows where executions took place until the 18th century, often providing entertainment for the jeering mob.

The ★ **Covenanters' Memorial ❶**, where the gibbet stood, was created in 1937, recalling the many martyrs who died for their faith alongside common criminals. The hanging of religious dissenters peaked in the 1680s under Catholic James II, but the original Covenanters were signatories of the National Covenant of 1638, opposing imposition of the English form of Protestantism *(see page 38)*. At West Bow, where the well stands, the wide Grassmarket splits into narrower roads. The **Cowgate** runs east along the lower edge of the Old Town, beneath the high arches of George IV and South Bridges. Once a route for cattle on their way to the grazings on the Burgh Muir, the street became fashionable in the 16th century; by the 19th century, however, its tenements were immigrants' slum homes. Now it is liveliest after dark, being packed with nightclubs.

GEORGE IV BRIDGE

Two streets at West Bow curve up to meet George IV Bridge. Candlemaker Row, sloping uphill

Star Attractions
● The Grassmarket
● Royal Mile

from the start of Cowgate, contains the **Hall of the Incorporation of Candlemakers**, built in 1722. Long ago farmers from the north and south would gather in the inns and taverns of this street. **Victoria Street**, noted for the individuality of its shops, is on the north side of West Bow and curves uphill to connect with the bridge, erected on nine arches by Thomas Hamilton in 1832.

The street emerges opposite the ★**National Library of Scotland** ❷ (Exhibition Hall: open June–Oct: Mon–Sat 10am–5pm, Sun 2–5pm; public access to reading rooms is restricted; free), which has the right to demand a copy of every book printed in the country.

From the top of George IV Bridge the vista ahead is of the imposing **Bank of Scotland** headquarters, built in 1806 and extended 60 years later. You are now on the ridge of the ★★★**Royal Mile**, the oldest thoroughfare in the city. The Lawnmarket section, up the hill from the bridge, is where the produce of the surrounding land, as well as wool and linen from 'landward' districts, was sold. A complex system of pends (vaulted passages), closes (entrances to tenement buildings) and wynds (alleyways) are found along the full length of the Royal Mile, often providing access to courtyards named after former inhabitants. **Brodie's Close**, on the left side going up the hill, recalls one of

Below: National Library
Bottom: looking down the
Royal Mile from the Castle

Map on pages 18–19

the city's more infamous sons, a town council-lor and cabinet-maker by day, a burglar by night.

THE LAWNMARKET

On the north side of the Lawnmarket, **Lady Stair's Close**, where Burns lodged in 1786, is named after its 18th-century owner; these days it's a ★ **Writers' Museum ❸** (open Mon–Sat: 10am–5pm, Sun during festival 2–5pm; free), containing relics belonging to Sir Walter Scott, Robert Burns and Robert Louis Stevenson, Scotland's best-known literary ambassadors. Paving stones, leading past the museum to the far end of the courtyard, have set into them quotations from the works of other Scottish writers.

Back on the Lawnmarket, next door is ★★ **Gladstone's Land ❹** (open daily; Good Fri–Oct: 10am–5pm, to 7pm in July and Aug), the six-storey home of a prosperous 17th century merchant. It is furnished with great authenticity to give an impression of life in Edinburgh's Old Town more than 300 years ago.

★ **Riddle's Court ❺**, across the road, dates from 1587 and contains the residence of Bailie John McMorran, a wealthy merchant shot dead by a schoolboy while trying to quell a riot at the Royal High School in 1595. In 1598, a banquet was held here for James VI and his queen, Anne

Below: Writers' Museum
Bottom: Gladstone's Land

of Denmark. The building, now serving as an educational centre, has a 16th-century painted ceiling and 17th-century plasterwork.

CASTLE HILL

On the far side of the mini-roundabout dividing the Lawnmarket from Castlehill, the top section of the Royal Mile, the former **Tolbooth St John's Church** has been transformed into **The Hub**, Edinburgh's Festival Centre with a ticket booth, shop and café (open Mon and Sun 9.30am–6pm, Tues–Sat 9.30am–late). The 19th-century church (where services used to be held in Gaelic), was designed by James Gillespie Graham and Augustus Pugin and has a 240-ft (73-metre) spire, the tallest in Edinburgh.

A tenement once said to have been occupied by the Laird o'Cockpen, a 17th-century lord provost, contains the ★★ **Camera Obscura and World of Illuminations** ❻ (open daily; Apr–Oct: 9.30am–6pm; July and Aug: late opening; Nov–Mar: 10am–5pm) within the Outlook Tower, added on by the architect Patrick Geddes in the 19th century. The Camera provides live images of the surrounding city, including close-ups of stone-masonry you couldn't otherwise view. Other attractions include eye-deceiving holograms.

RAMSAY GARDENS

In front of the castle esplanade, a fountain and plaque marks the spot where witches and warlocks were burned from the 16th to 18th centuries, after being half drowned in the Nor' Loch. A short diversion to the right, down steep, cobbled Ramsay Lane, leads to **Ramsay Garden**, a delightful residential complex also built by Sir Patrick Geddes, which contained the homes of that fine Scottish poet Allan Ramsay (1686–1758) and his painter son, also Allan Ramsay (1713–84).

Follow the street around the corner for open scenic views over the New Town towards the Firth of Forth, and to see the ★ **Assembly Hall** ❼, designed by William Playfair. Every May this is

Star Attractions
- **Gladstone's Land**
- **Camera Obscura**

Canonball House
The old building next to the Whisky Centre dates from 1630 and is named after the iron shot imbedded in the west gable; according to legend, this was fired from the castle ramparts during the Jacobite siege of 1745.

The Camera Obscura on Castle Hill

Map
on pages
18–19

the meeting place of the General Assembly of the Church of Scotland, and was the home of the Scottish Parliament debating chamber until 2004 (for details of access, tel: 0131-651 2189). The building also contains **New College**, for students of theology at Edinburgh University.

Nearing the top of Castlehill is the ★★**Scotch Whisky Heritage Centre** ❽ (open daily; May–Sept: 9.30am–6.30pm; Oct–Apr: 10am–6pm; closed 25 Dec; last tour 1 hour before closing time). A tour lasting about an hour provides a thorough briefing on whisky, with a free dram. Across the road is the **Tartan Weaving Mill and Exhibition** where visitors can try their hand at weaving on a functional mill.

THE CASTLE

Perched high on an extinct volcanic outcrop and dominating the skyline is ★★★**Edinburgh Castle** ❾ (open daily; Apr–Sept: 9.30am–6pm; Oct–Mar: 9.30am–5pm; steward guided tours and audio tours; closed 25–26 Dec). On the esplanade each August is held the Edinburgh Military Tattoo, one of the great spectacles of the festival season.

Edinburgh Castle has withstood many sieges and occupations in its 1,000-year history. Recent excavations have unearthed evidence of Iron-Age and Dark-Age forts, suggesting the site was occu-

Edinburgh Castle

pied in 850BC. Malcolm III and his Saxon queen, Margaret, lived here in the 11th century, after which it became a frequent retreat for the Scottish monarchy. After five centuries of attacks by the English, it is remarkable that so much of it has survived. From the 12th century, every occupant modified or added to the original structure, so that today it is a rich architectural mix of palace, fortress, barracks, chapel and war memorial.

Star Attractions
● Scotch Whisky Centre
● Edinburgh Castle

CASTLE TOUR

Enter across the modern **drawbridge** and **gatehouse**. Ahead is the great parapet of the **Half-Moon Battery**, built by Regent Morton in 1574 on the ruins of the 14th-century David's Tower. The path then leads towards the **Portcullis Gate**, from the same period.

Interior of the Great Hall, Edinburgh Castle

Next door to the 18th-century **Queen Anne Building** in Crown Square is the ★★**Scottish National War Memorial**. It was designed in 1927 by Sir Robert Lorimer, and contains the names of the dead of two world wars. On the south side of the square is the ★**Great Hall** which dates from the 16th century. Today it is used for ceremonial occasions, dramatised by the hammerbeam ceiling with its ornate carvings. Also in the square is the 15th-century ★**Palace**. In the royal apartments on the ground floor is **Queen Mary's Room**, where in 1566 Mary Queen of Scots gave birth to James VI of Scotland (also James I of England).

★★★ **The Crown Room** on the first floor displays the **Honours of Scotland**. The Scottish crown is one of the oldest in Europe, said to date from the reign of Robert I in the 14th century, but with arches from an older crown. The sceptre was a gift from Pope Alexander VI to King James IV in 1494, and the sword of state was a present to that same king by Pope Julius II.

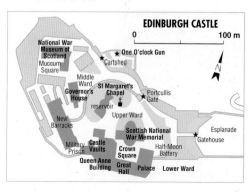

EDINBURGH CASTLE

0   100 m

National War
Museum of
Scotland
Mucoum
Square

One O'clock Gun
Cartshed

Middle
Ward
Governor's
House

St Margaret's
Chapel

Portcullis
Gate

reservoir

Upper Ward

New
Barracks

Scottish National
War Memorial

Esplanade

Military
Prison

Castle
Vaults

Crown
Square

Half-Moon
Battery

Gatehouse

Queen Anne
Building

Great
Hall

Palace

Lower Ward

N

Map
on pages
18–19

Crag and tail

The Castle is built on volcanic rock that survived the last Ice Age and protected a ridge of rock behind it from advancing glaciers. The resulting 'crag and tail' created a site for a well-protected town on raised ground between two valleys and beneath the towering fortress. The Royal Mile is so named because it runs the length of the 'tail' for 1 mile 106 yards, from one royal dwelling, the Castle, to another, the Palace of Holyroodhouse.

St Margaret Window,
St Margaret's Chapel

When Oliver Cromwell occupied Scotland in 1651, the Scottish regalia were removed for safe keeping. They lay buried in a churchyard until the Restoration when they were returned to the castle. It was not until 1822, when King George IV announced that he was to visit his Scottish subjects, that the honours were put on display. Also in the Crown Room is the **Stone of Destiny** (or Stone of Scone), the traditional coronation seat of Scottish monarchs which was stolen by English king Edward I 700 years ago, and not returned until 1996.

ST MARGARET'S CHAPEL

Beside the **reservoir** is the oldest building in the castle (and in Edinburgh), the 12th-century ★★ **St Margaret's Chapel,** said to have been built by David I in honour of his mother, Queen Margaret, who died in 1093. The stained glass windows, one featuring a likeness of Margaret, were inserted into the existing openings in the 1920s. On the ramparts in front of the chapel is **Mons Meg**, a 6-tonne (7,700kg) cannon allegedly employed at the siege of Norham in the 15th century.

On the left of the **New Barracks** (1796) on the west side of the castle are the **Military Prison** and **Castle Vaults**, where prisoners of war were held in the 18th and 19th centuries. On the right of the New Barracks is the ★**National War Museum of Scotland** in the former Ordnance Storehouse and Hospital, either side of Museum Square above the exposed Western Defences. Displays explore the nation's military history and the life of the soldier.

The **Governor's House** in the Middle Ward was built in 1742 as the Castle Governor's official residence, and it now houses the Army Officers' Mess with magnificent views over the city from the Jacobite Dining Room.

One of the best-known features of Edinburgh Castle is the **One O'clock Gun**, fired from the ramparts daily at 1pm except Sunday. True natives of Edinburgh, wherever they are in the world, will always start and look at their watches at one o'clock. The gun is on Mills Mount Battery beside the **Redcoat Café**, now a self-service café.

2: Old Town and Palace

St Giles Cathedral – John Knox House – Canongate Tolbooth – Palace of Holyroodhouse – Holyrood Park

The route begins by the cathedral at the top of the High Street and leads down the **Royal Mile** to the Queen's Edinburgh residence and new Parliament, and the semi-wild park behind.

Much of Scotland's turbulent history was enacted along the Royal Mile, a sequence of four streets between Edinburgh Castle and the Palace of Holyroodhouse. Route 1 covered Castle Hill and the Lawnmarket; we can now progress along the **High Street** and the Canongate.

HEART OF MIDLOTHIAN

On the pavement in front of the west door of the St Giles Cathedral is the **Heart of Midlothian**, a heart-shape worked into the cobbles, inspired by the celebrated novel of that name by Sir Walter Scott and signifying the centre of the district in which it stands. Here stood the Old (1438) and New Tolbooths, the city's administrative centres, at one time the parliament and law courts, and latterly the town jail and place of execution. As a consequence, the cobbled heart is traditionally spat upon by passers-by to show their contempt.

Map on pages 18–19

Star Attraction
● St Margaret's Chapel

Below: Royal Mile street signs
Bottom: Heart of Midlothian

Below: Strachein's window, St Giles Cathedral (bottom)

The outline of a building, which jutted into the road, is marked by brass plates. It was demolished in 1817 to allow the street to be widened and unblock the view of the cathedral, or High Kirk. The original Tolbooth gateway, door and padlock were acquired by Sir Walter Scott for use at Abbotsford, the house he built for himself in the Borders. Adjoining the Tolbooth, in front of the cathedral, were 'luckenbooths', a row of shops also pulled down in 1817.

The statue nearby is the 5th Duke of Buccleuch, Lord President of the Council in 1846, who built the harbour at Granton. Across the road, in classical robes, sits David Hume, the 18th-century philosopher and atheist who lived in Edinburgh.

ST GILES

The ★★★ **St Giles Cathedral** ⑩ (open Mon–Sat 9am–5pm, to 7pm weekdays in summer, Sun 1–5pm; free) sits on the site of a building erected during the reign of Alexander I (1107–24). This, the Church of Scotland's principal kirk, comprises architecture dating from the 12th century. The crown of St Giles was added in the 16th century, and the spire is supported by eight flying buttresses and topped with a golden weathercock dating from 1567. John Knox, the great Scottish reformer, became its first Protestant minister after the Reformation, and a modern statue of him stands close to the west door. Charles I made St Giles a cathedral in 1633 by appointing a bishop, but attempts to introduce a new English prayer book alien to Scottish Presbyterianism resulted in riots. The bishop was removed in 1638, but the continuing conflict between the religious Scots and their remote rulers contributed to the outbreak of the English Civil War. Bishops were reintroduced at the Restoration in 1660, when Jenny Geddes, a local housewife, is said to have thrown her folding-stool at the preacher in St Giles. The bishop was ejected 18 years later and the cathedral reverted to its proper title of High Kirk.

CATHEDRAL TREASURES

The cathedral's interior has beautiful 19th- and 20th-century stained glass, splendid military and civilian memorials, and a fine organ, designed by Rieger Orgelbau. The West Window is in memory of the poet Robert Burns; the Montrose and Argyll windows bear the arms of the protagonists of the Covenanting period, who opposed the enforcement of an English religion on Scotland (*see page 38*); the windows in the Moray Aisle depict the funeral of the Regent Moray, Mary Queen of Scots' illegitimate half-brother who was assassinated in Linlithgow. A shop and a restaurant are situated in the Lower Aisle.

The greatest honour in Scottish life is to be made a Knight of the Thistle, the personal gift of a monarch. It is the equivalent of England's Order of the Garter, and at any one time there are no more than 16 holders. ★★ **The Thistle Chapel**, which sits on one side of the cathedral, was a gift from John David, 12th Earl of Leven and 11th Earl of Melville, and designed by Sir Robert Lorimer. Built between 1909 and 1911, it is perhaps the most ornate post-medieval building of its size in Scotland. The knights' stalls are carved in oak in a light and elegant Gothic style, and the original heraldic stall plates were enamelled by Phoebe Traquair.

Star Attractions
- **St Giles Cathedral**
- **Thistle Chapel**

Side steps
It is well worth exploring some of the closes, or narrow passageways, off the Royal Mile, which retain centuries-old features. Typically, in Advocates Close, at the top of the High Street, a door lintel is carved with a religious motto and the intertwined initials of the owner and his wife, and the remains of a turnpike staircase that served the tall tenement can be seen. Here, the impressive DOM art gallery occupies one of the city's oldest houses.

Thistle Chapel ceiling, St Giles Cathedral

Map on pages 18–19

Mary King's Close
For some years local historians have run guided tours of this fascinating hidden close, which is believed to be haunted by plague victims. There have been several sightings of a crying little girl in ragged clothes.

Mercat Cross, St Giles Cathedral

PARLIAMENT HALL

From the west steps of St Giles, the ★ **Signet Library** stands to the left, adjoining the **Advocates Library** and ★ ★ **Parliament Hall** ⓫ (open Mon–Fri 10am–4pm; access from No. 11; free), which front onto Parliament Square, behind St Giles. The Renaissance Parliament House had a facelift in the early 19th century (hence the false windows on the Georgian facade), and today it provides chambers for the judges of Scotland's Court of Session, advocates and barristers, who may be seen pacing the Hall in their gowns and wigs. Here, in this present-day bastion of tradition, the old Scottish parliament met until the 1707 Act of Union brought together Scotland and England. The Hall is 122ft (37 metres) long and 60ft (18 metres) high, with a 49-ft (15-metre) wide hammerbeam ceiling of dark oak. The stained-glass south windows by Wilhelm von Kaulbach depict the inauguration of the College of Justice by James V.

The interior of the adjoining 19th-century Signet Library houses the books of the Society of Writers to H.M. Signet, Scotland's legal fraternity. The vaulted salon of the upper library is often used for concerts and receptions. The ceiling carries Thomas Stotland's 1821 painting of Apollo and the Muses. In Parliament Square is the oldest equestrian statue in Britain, depicting (with some artistic licence) Charles II wearing the robes of a Roman emperor.

MERCAT CROSS

On the east side of St Giles is the ★ **Mercat Cross**, from which proclamations are still made on State occasions. The original cross was virtually destroyed in the 18th century, but a small part of its shaft was incorporated into this 1885 replica. The cross marks a traditional trading place and site of public tortures. The capital and the eight medallions proclaim the royal arms of Britain, Scotland, England and Ireland in company with the arms of Edinburgh, Leith, Canongate and Edinburgh University.

Immediately across the High Street, through arches which once contained shop booths, are the ★ **City Chambers**, designed by John Adam but built by John Fergus in the mid-18th century. They were taken over by the Town Council in 1811, having formerly been used as a Royal Exchange housing commercial offices. A statue of Bucephalus being restrained by Alexander, sculpted by Sir John Steell, stands in the forecourt.

Underneath the City Chambers a warren of streets in what were the lower levels of the original Old Town has been uncovered. Notable is ★ **Mary King's Close** which, in 1645, was sealed off following an outbreak of plague in which hundreds died. It was recently re-opened (open daily; Apr–Oct: 10am–9pm; Nov–Mar: 10am–4pm; entry from Warriston's Close) and the past is brought to life with dramatic episodes and apparitions.

At No. 180 High Street is the **Festival Fringe Society office** (open Mon–Fri 10am–5.30pm, Sat 10am–5pm; extended hours and Sun during Festival; shop) where tickets for the annual Festival Fringe shows can be purchased. At the junction with North and South Bridges is the **Tron Kirk ⓬**, built by John Mylne in 1637–48 but reduced in size to make way for the latter bridge and Hunter Square 140 years later. It is named after the 'tron' salt-weighing beam that once stood on the site. The original steeple was consumed in 1824, by a fire that destroyed a swathe of the south side of the High Street. Unused for worship since 1952, the Tron Kirk currently contains an

Star Attractions
● **Parliament Hall**
● **Mary King's Close**

Below: Tron Kirk
Bottom: City Chambers statue of Alexander the Great

Map on pages 18–19

Old Town information centre and exhibition (open June–Oct: daily 10am–5pm; free). Inside, archaeologists have uncovered one of the city's oldest streets under the floor, which can be viewed.

MUSEUM OF CHILDHOOD

Beyond the Tron Kirk, the High Street broadens and continues its downward slope towards Holyrood. The turreted building to the right is the **Crowne Plaza Hotel**, built in 1989 in the vernacular style. Lower down the street, on the same side, is the ★★ **Museum of Childhood** ⓭ (open Mon–Sat 10am–5pm; Sun afternoons in July and Aug; free). It was the world's first museum on this theme and has a significant collection of historical toys, dolls and books.

★ **Tweeddale Court** was once the home of the 1st Marquis of Tweeddale, Chancellor of Scotland in 1692. One of the restored courtyard buildings houses the **Saltire Society**, a group which seeks to promote and preserve Scottish culture.

Opposite, in Chalmers Close, is ★ **The Brass Rubbing Centre** (open Apr–Sept: Mon–Sat 10am–5pm; Sun during Edinburgh Festival, noon–5pm; free). The centre occupies Trinity Apse, the remnant of what was the finest collegiate church in Scotland (founded 1460). There is a collection of replicas moulded from ancient

Down in the dungeon
A diversion from the High Street, down Cockburn Street towards Waverley Station and right along Market Street, will take you to an attraction that brings to life the darker practices of olden times. In the Edinburgh Dungeon (open daily 10am–5pm, extended hours in summer) actors recreate gruesome crimes and punishments, and there's a mind-boggling collection of medieval torture instruments – so it's best not to take little ones.

Museum of Childhood

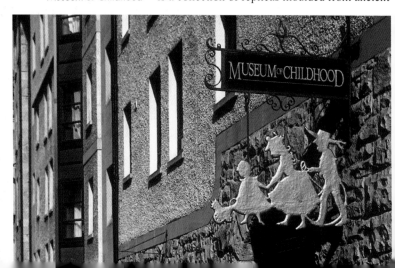

Pictish stones, and rare Scottish and medieval brasses (there is a charge for rubbings).

OLDEST HOUSE

Moubray House, restored by the Cockburn Society in 1910, is probably the oldest occupied dwelling in Edinburgh, recorded as far back as 1477. Daniel Defoe, author of *Robinson Crusoe*, edited the *Edinburgh Courant* from here in 1710.

Next door, **John Knox House ⓮** (open Mon–Sat 10am–6pm; July and Aug: Sun noon–5pm; re-opens after renovation in early summer 2005) dates from around 1490 and contains relics associated with the religious reformer. It is doubtful he ever lived here, but there is evidence to suggest he preached from the bow window. More accurately, it was the home of James Mossman, goldsmith to Mary Queen of Scots.

The adjacent **Netherbow Arts Centre** comprises a small theatre, gallery space and café on the site of Netherbow Port, the original east gate to the city, demolished in 1764. Here, at the junction with Jeffrey Street and St Mary's Street, you cross into the **Canongate**, which was once a separate burgh (town).

THE CANONGATE

★ **The People's Story ⓯** (open Mon–Sat 10am–5pm; Sun during Festival 2–5pm) is a museum that tells of citizens' lives over the past 200 years with sounds, sights and smells. It occupies the ★ **Canongate Tolbooth**, which is readily recognisable by its distinctive clock tower overhanging the pavement. It was built in 1591 for use as a courthouse, prison and centre of municipal affairs.

On the south side of the Canongate, **Moray House**, built in 1628, served as Oliver Cromwell's headquarters during a stay in Edinburgh. The Marquess of Argyll reputedly watched from the balcony as his rival Montrose passed by to his execution in 1650. **Huntly House**, a fine example of a restored 16th-century mansion, houses the city's principal museum of local history, the

Star Attraction
● **Museum of Childhood**

Below: John Knox House and (bottom) detail

Map on pages 18–19

Map on pages 18–19

The canon's gait
While Edinburgh expanded by creeping down the hill from the Castle, the burgh of Canongate, or 'canon's road', developed separately under the auspices of Holyrood Abbey. Many Scots nobles had homes along the Canongate, and some fine 17th-century mansions survive. The two towns were separated by the Flodden Wall and Netherbow Port, and those living outside the boundary of Edinburgh were unprotected from attack.

Queen Mary's Bath-house

★ **Museum of Edinburgh** (open Mon–Sat 10am–5pm; Sun during Edinburgh Festival, 2–5pm; free), containing important collections of glass, pottery, shop signs, the original National Covenant and relics relating to Field Marshall Earl Haig, the infamous World War I general.

CANONGATE KIRK

★★ **Canongate Kirk** ⑯, on the north side, was built to serve the congregation ousted from the Abbey Church of Holyrood in 1691, when the latter was converted into a Catholic chapel for the Knights of the Thistle by James VII (James II of England). The Queen now worships here when in the city. In its graveyard lie Adam Smith, the economist who wrote *The Wealth of Nations*, Horatius Bonar, the hymn writer, and the young poet Robert Fergusson, who was so much admired by Robert Burns that he erected a stone over Fergusson's unmarked grave.

The last stretch of the Canongate is dominated by the new Scottish Parliament building (*see page 37*) on the south side. On the north side, set back from the street, is **Whitehorse Close**, an attractive courtyard of buildings dating from the 17th century. In the 18th century, stagecoaches travelling to London would depart from the White Horse Inn.

At the foot of the Canongate stands **Queen Mary's Bath-house**, a quaintly shaped 16th-century bothy. Although it carries this name, there's no historical evidence to suggest that the Queen ever made use of it. Beside it are the gates of the Palace of Holyroodhouse and Abbey Strand, comprising two 16th-century houses.

HOLYROODHOUSE

The ★★ **Palace of Holyroodhouse** ⑰ (usually open daily but tel: 0131-556 5100 to check; Apr–Oct: 9.30am–6pm; Nov–Mar: 9.30am–4.30pm), the Queen's Edinburgh home, is among the most ancient of the residences still occupied by the British royal family. Founded in 1128 by King David I as an abbey for Augustinian canons, it takes its name from a relic believed to have been

a segment from Christ's cross (*rood* means cross).
It was transformed into a royal palace in the 16th
century. All that remains of the original Holyroodhouse is the ruined nave of the ★ **Abbey
Church**, which also served Edinburgh congre-
gations and then became a royal chapel. Its
destruction was caused in part by Orangemen who
purged it of its Catholic ornamentation after the
bloodless revolution of 1688. The south aisle contains the remains of several kings.

At the turn of the 16th century, part of the abbey
compound was made into a royal residence for
James IV and his consort Margaret Tudor. James
V built the tower-like northwestern corner. A
range to the west completed the palace when
Mary, his daughter, took up residence with her
second husband, Lord Darnley. Holyrood is
closely associated with Mary Queen of Scots: her
secretary, David Rizzio, was brutally murdered
here in 1566. Darnley himself died when a bomb
exploded in the nearby residence of Kirk O'Field.

ROYAL PATRONS

Despite its bloody history, Mary's son, James VI,
made full use of the building before he departed
to London in 1603. He returned for one brief visit,
and said in London: 'This I may say of Scotland,
and may truly vaunt it; here I sit and govern it with

Star Attractions
● **Canongate Kirk**
● **Palace of Holyroodhouse**

*Below: Palace of
Holyroodhouse and (bottom)
its Morning Drawing Room*

Map on pages 18–19

Below: the Queen's Antechamber, Holyrood
Bottom: Arthur's Seat

my pen. I write and it is done, and by a Clerk of the Council I govern Scotland now, which others could not do by the sword.'

It was his grandson, Charles II, crowned King of Scots at Scone in 1651, who truly established Holyrood as Scotland's royal residence. Though he never lived there, he oversaw its reconstruction with a new facade and lavish decoration. For a time, the future James VII (James II of England), Charles's brother, took up residence in the palace. In 1745, Prince Charles Edward Stuart (Bonnie Prince Charlie) occupied Holyrood for a short time before his victory at the Battle of Prestonpans, which was part of his campaign to win back the British throne for his father, the *de jure* James VIII (James III of England). Charles II lavishly furnished the drawing rooms and the state rooms, which have fine plasterwork ceilings. The portraits in the long Picture Gallery are a curiosity. They are supposedly Scottish monarchs, but the 111 likenesses by Jacob de Witt all resemble Charles II, who commissioned them, and more than 30 of them probably never existed.

The ★ **Queen's Gallery**, situated in front of the palace, features changing exhibits from the priceless Royal collection. Monarchists will adore the shop (open daily 9.30am–4.30pm or 6pm in summer).

HOLYROOD PARK

The parkland behind the road is the royal estate of ★★ **Holyrood Park** ⓭, 640 acres (260 hectares) of ground encircled by Queen's Drive, and dominated by a volcanic mini-mountain known as **Arthur's Seat**. A few hundred yards/metres east of the palace are St Margaret's Loch and, nearby, the 15th-century **St Margaret's Well**. Above the loch stand the ruins of **St Anthony's Chapel**, a medieval monastery.

A footpath leads towards the ascent to 822-ft (250-metre) high Arthur's Seat and **Salisbury Crags**, a steep ridge where a path below the upper cliffs is known as the **Radical Road**, because impoverished radical weavers under the direction of Sir Walter Scott built it in the 1820s. Arthur's Seat probably takes its name from a prince of Strathclyde in the Dark Ages, and Salisbury Crags from the English commander who rested his troops here in the early 14th century.

SCOTTISH PARLIAMENT

The Queen opened the controversial **Scottish Parliament building**, (open Mon-Fri, 10am-6pm, Weekends 10am-4pm) in October 2004. It was designed by a Catalan, the late Enric Miralles, and construction began in 1999. The cost of the project spiralled to more than £400 million – when it was initially claimed the price tag would be a mere £40 million. However, since completion the building has won a clutch of prestigious architecture awards. It appears to grow organically from the city's slopes while bringing something refreshing and radical to Edinburgh's skyline. To truly feel the force of this work, though, you have to get inside and take a tour. Access is free.

Afterwards pop across the road to the hugely popular ★★ **Our Dynamic Earth** (open Apr–Oct: daily 10am–6pm; Nov–Mar: Wed–Sun 10am–5pm), to experience earthquakes, ice ages and tropical rainstorms. See, hear, feel and smell the planet as it was millions of years ago.

★

Star Attractions
● Holyrood Park
● Queen's Gallery
● Our Dynamic Earth

Savouring the servants
At the northwest end of the new Parliament compound a much older building, Queensbury House, has been incorporated. It was built in 1681 and soon after sold to the 1st Duke of Queensferry, one of the chief promoters of the Treaty of Union in 1707. His inbred son, Lord Drumlanrig, was found in the kitchen here eating a servant boy whom he had roasted on the spit, apparently having escaped his restraints while the rest of the household was witnessing the signing of the Union.

Futuristic building of Our Dynamic Earth

Map on pages 18–19

Covenanter's prison

In 1638, hundreds of citizens, including many noblemen, flocked to the Greyfriars to sign the National Covenant. Its supporters, known as Covenanters, took issue with the imposition on the Scottish people of the English doctrines of Episcopacy. In 1679, 1,200 of them were imprisoned in cruel conditions for more than five months in an enclosure now incorporated into the kirkyard, which may still be seen. Many of those who survived were subsequently transported to the colonies to be sold into slavery.

Statue of Greyfriars Bobby

3: The South Side

Greyfriars – Museum of Scotland – Old College – Edinburgh Festival Theatre – Royal Commonwealth Pool – Duddingston

This route begins at the statue of Greyfriar's Bobby and proceeds via the two national museums in Chambers Street, turning south along the A7 to take in the university district. You may wish to end the tour at the Surgeons' Hall or take a bus from there to the attractions further afield (Nos. 14, 30 and 33 go to the Commonwealth Pool, and No. 2 goes to Duddingston).

GREYFRIARS

The ★★ **Kirk of the Greyfriars** is situated at the top of Candlemaker Row as it runs uphill from the Grassmarket, and takes its name from the medieval Franciscan friary which stood on this spot. Among those buried in the churchyard are George Buchanan, tutor to James VI, the Earl of Morton, Regent of Scotland from 1572 to 1578, William Adam, the architect, Allan Ramsay, the poet, Duncan Ban Macintyre, the Gaelic poet, and William Smellie, who edited the *Encyclopaedia Britannica*.

On the corner of George IV Bridge and Candlemaker Row is the tiny statue of **Greyfriars Bobby ⑲**, the little Skye terrier who so faithfully visited his master's grave in Greyfriars churchyard each day for 14 years, and who was immortalised by Walt Disney. On his death in 1872, he was buried near to his master, just inside the entrance to the churchyard.

JINGLIN' GEORDIE

Immediately behind the Kirk of the Greyfriars is **George Heriot's School**, endowed by and named after the goldsmith, 'Jinglin' Geordie', who accompanied James VI to London. He became a moneylender and amassed a large fortune which he left for the care and education of orphan boys. The school was built in 1660 by

William Wallace and William Ayton, and subsequently improved by John and Robert Mylne. It is now co-educational. Across Lauriston Place is the late 19th century Royal Infirmary of Edinburgh (since moved to new buildings at Little France), the work of John and David Bryce.

Linking up to George IV Bridge on the east side is **Chambers Street**, dating from an 1860s improvement scheme. It is named after the Lord Provost of the time, William Chambers, who founded the publishing company which still bears his name and whose statue stands in the centre of the street. On the north side, the former Heriot-Watt University building is now the **Sheriff Courthouse**.

NATIONAL MUSEUMS

Opposite the Courthouse stands the imposing sandstone-clad ★★★ **Museum of Scotland** ❷⓿ (open Mon–Sat 10am–5pm, Tues to 8pm; Sun noon–5pm; free), completed in 1998 to bring under one roof some of Scotland's most valuable national treasures and tell the country's history from earliest times to the present day. Artefacts on display range from Pictish gravestones to the famous 12th-century Lewis chesspieces, and silverware belonging to Charles Edward Stuart. An impressive narrative is woven around the objects.

Star Attractions
● **Kirk of Greyfriars**
● **Museum of Scotland**

Below: Museum of Scotland and (bottom) the tomb of Mary Queen of Scots inside

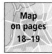

Map on pages 18–19

Below: steam train in the Museum of Scotland Bottom: interior of the Royal Museum

Next door is the magnificent 19th-century ★★★ **Royal Museum** (open Mon–Sat 10am–5pm, Tues to 8pm; Sun noon–5pm; free).Designed by Francis Fowke, it was built between 1861 and 1885. The 270-ft (82-metre) main hall, which is roofed in glass, is often used for receptions and banquets. The Royal Museum has a superb international collection including natural history and fossils, scientific implements, Asiatic sculpture and Chinese and Islamic decorative art. The two adjoining museums are the largest in the UK outside London.

THE UNIVERSITY

Next to the Royal Museum is the University of Edinburgh's **Old College** ㉑, the front of which lies on South Bridge. The foundation stone was laid in 1789 but the building, to Robert Adam's design, was only completed in 1834 by William Playfair, who was responsible for the interior designs. The dome, surmounted by a small statue of a 'golden boy' carrying the torch of knowledge, was added in 1879.

The **Talbot Rice Gallery** (open Tues–Sat 10am–5pm; Sun during Edinburgh Festival; free) in the college is a popular venue for contemporary art exhibitions. It also has a small permanent collection of Old Masters and bronzes.

James VI granted a charter to found a college in Edinburgh in 1582, and the University was built on the site of Kirk o' Field, where pre-Reformation monasteries had been and where the Old College stands. Its present situation resulted from the vision of Lord Provost George Drummond, who masterminded improvements to the South Side as well as the creation of the New Town.

The University buildings of **George Square** and the **McEwan Hall**, used for graduation ceremonies and functions, range behind the Old College. George Square was begun in the late 18th century by James Brown, who named it after his brother. It was largely bulldozed by the university in the central redevelopment plan of the 1960s, but the west side and part of the east side remain intact.

Under South Bridge
Two landmarks rise up from either end of the South Bridge: the Tron Kirk and Old College. But you can only tell you're on a bridge by peering down at the Cowgate from above the single open archway. The buildings lining it are not on the bridge but flush with it, with basements in the valley below, and the other 18 arches of the South Bridge, built in 1785–88 to link the Old Town with the University, contain vaulted chambers once used as workshops and cellars. Mercat Tours operate guided tours of the vaults (daily; tel: 0131-557 6464 for details).

FESTIVAL THEATRE

Beyond the South Bridge on Nicolson Street is the glass-fronted ★ **Edinburgh Festival Theatre** ㉒ (tel: 0131-529 6000), converted from the old Empire Theatre in 1994 by architects Law & Dunbar-Nasmith. Several theatres have occupied this site. The one that caught fire in 1811 caused the death on stage of the Great Lafayette, a celebrated illusionist. The present structure has 2,000 seats and a stage area larger than that of the Royal Opera House in Covent Garden, London.

MEDICAL MUSEUMS

Opposite is the ★ **Royal College of Surgeons of Edinburgh** ㉓ (the **Surgeon's Hall**), again the work of William Playfair. The Playfair Hall at the front contains a ★ **Museum of Pathology and Anatomy** (viewing, including guided tours of the College and Museum, by appointment, tel: 0131-527 1649) where there is a collection of anatomical parts. Adjacent, at No. 9 Hill Square, are the College's **Dental Museum**, including the Menzies Campbell Collection, and the **Jules Thorn Exhibition of the History of Surgery** (both open Mon–Fri noon–4pm; free), which illustrates how recently practices we now take

Edinburgh Festival Theatre

Map on pages 18–19

Burke and Hare

The University's Anatomy Department achieved notoriety as well as recognition for its pioneering work in the early 19th century, when some professors purchased corpses for their dissection classes at the same time as recently buried coffins went missing from nearby graveyards. In 1828 William Burke and William Hare went a step further than the body-snatchers by murdering the specimens they supplied to Dr Knox. The former was hanged for his crimes in front of a crowd of 20,000, and his skin was flayed and sold. Burke's skeleton is in the Anatomy Department's collection at Teviot Place.

Raeburn's portrayal of skating on Duddingston Loch

for granted have developed. The original Royal Infirmary was sited nearby from the early 18th century (remembered in Infirmary Street, opposite the Old College), and the University's renowned medical school grew in tandem with it.

QUEEN'S HALL

Much further along this route, on Clerk Street, is the **Queen's Hall**, a Georgian church designed by Robert Brown in 1823. It hosts a wide range of mainly classical concerts and entertainments throughout the year (tel: 0131-668 2019).

At the end of Clerk Street, the road to the right leads to the **Meadows**. A Burgh Loch before the 18th century, the Meadows were reclaimed during the Enlightenment by Thomas Hope of Rankeillour, the president of the Society of Improvers of the Knowledge of Agriculture in Scotland. They opened as a public park in 1860 and are now a green space providing a range of facilities.

The road to the left (east) connects with Dalkeith Road, where the Scottish Widows Fund & Life Assurance Society occupies a striking, hexagonal building faced in dark glass. A short distance from here is the **Royal Commonwealth Pool** **24** (tel: 0131-667 7211 for opening times), built for the 1970 Commonwealth Games. It has a sauna, weight-training facilities and an Olympic-sized pool. Next door are the University of Edinburgh's Pollock Halls of Residence.

DUDDINGSTON

To the northeast, approached through the park, is the well-preserved ★ **Duddingston Village**, named for a 12th-century Norman knight called Dodin, who leased the land from the Abbot of Kelso. **Duddingston Kirk** dates from the 12th century, with later additions, and **Duddingston Loch** – where Sir Henry Raeburn set his famous portrait of the Rev. Robert Walker skating – is now a bird sanctuary.

The **Sheep's Heid Inn** dates from the 16th century when James VI is said to have presented the owner with a silver ram's head.

4: East to Calton Hill

St Mary's Roman Catholic Cathedral – Calton Hill – Waterloo Place – Scott Monument

This route begins in front of St Mary's Cathedral at the east end of the New Town, and scales Calton Hill. From the Scott Monument there are city-wide views.

Map on pages 18–19

PICARDY PLACE

St Mary's Roman Catholic Cathedral ㉕ (open daily 8.30am–6pm; free), designed by James Gillespie Graham in 1813, was the first Catholic church to be built in Edinburgh after the Reformation. A fire in 1878 left only the facade, but the early 20th-century nave is interesting. On the terracing in front of the cathedral, facing Picardy Place roundabout, three statues include a giant foot and a hand by Sir Eduardo Paolozzi, born in 1924 in nearby Leith. These symbolise the strong connections between Edinburgh and the Italian families from Bargos and Monte Cassino, who arrived at the end of the 19th century.

Leith Street, connecting Picardy Place with Princes Street, is straddled by a shopping centre, the architecturally derided 1960s **St James Centre**, and a new leisure complex with multiscreen cinema and health club. Its glass-panel

Below: the Scott Monument
Bottom: sculpture in front of St Mary's Cathedral

Map
on pages
18–19

style typifies the many recently-built office and leisure developments, which tend to dwarf older buildings, in the currently burgeoning city. Next to the new centre, on Leith Walk, is the ★**Playhouse Theatre** (tel: 0870-606 3424), the city's largest venue for live entertainment. Nearby is another reminder of Edinburgh's rich Italian heritage, the famous delicatessen and restaurant **Valvona and Crolla** (0131-556 6066).

CALTON HILL

★★★**Calton Hill** is a volcanic outcrop (like Arthur's Seat) at the east end of the New Town. It may be approached via Greenside Lane, adjoining the theatre (which first descends and then links with a path leading up), but the more attractive route climbs the steep, cobbled road (also called Calton Hill) on its west side; this connects with Waterloo Place and a path to the summit. From the top there are panoramic views of the Old and New Towns, Holyrood Palace, Arthur's Seat and the Firth of Forth. In summer this is a favourite dropping-off point for tourist coaches. (There is also car access from Royal Terrace and limited parking at the top.) Much of the building around the top of the hill and below dates from just after the Napoleonic Wars, in which Scottish soldiers played a significant role.

Below: National Monument on Calton Hill and (bottom) night view from the hill

CALTON MONUMENTS

On the south side of the hill is the ★**Nelson Monument** ㉖ (open Apr–Sept: Mon 1–6pm, Tues–Sat 10am–6pm; Oct–Mar: Mon–Sat 10am–3pm), erected in 1807 to celebrate Admiral Nelson's naval victory at Trafalgar. It's worth climbing the spiral staircase to the lookout platform on a clear day for the great views. The one o'clock Time Ball is dropped to coincide with the gun fired from Edinburgh Castle. With its sights trained on the length of Princes Street, a cannon squats defensively nearby, and to the west, the **Dugald Stewart Monument**, by William Playfair, commemorates a distinguished professor of philosophy at Edinburgh University.

Crowning the summit is **Rock House**, the 19th-century home of the pioneering photographer David Octavius Hill.

On the centre of the hill, the dozen pillars of the ★**National Monument** ㉗ honour the soldiers killed in the Napoleonic Wars. It was intended that this should be a full-scale replica of the Parthenon in Athens, but only the west side was completed before funds ran out. This side faces towards the former **City Observatory** ㉘, which has a Grecian-style dome and was designed by Sir William Playfair in 1818.

Star Attraction
● Calton Hill

> **Sleuth's creator**
> Located on the north side of Picardy Place is a statue of Sherlock Holmes by Gerald Ogilvy Laing. This commemorates the birth in 1859 of Holmes's creator, Sir Arthur Conan Doyle, whose family occupied a now demolished tenement flat in the centre of the old square.

Dugald Stewart Monument

BELOW THE HILL

Immediately below Calton Hill on Regent Road is the **Old Royal High School**, a Greek Doric building designed by Thomas Hamilton in 1829. Further along Regent Road, on the far side, is the 1830 Greek-temple style ★**Burns Monument**, again designed by Thomas Hamilton. It overlooks the **New Calton Burial Ground** ㉙, which dates from 1821.

Across the street from here, Regent Terrace curls around the slopes of Calton Hill to meet Royal Terrace, designed by Sir William Playfair, which features sets of seven, 10 and another seven giant Corinthian colonnades and balustrades, each set enclosing arched entrances and ground-floor windows.

Map on pages 18–19

Map on pages 18–19

Wages of Waterloo
The early 19th-century eastward expansion of the New Town was a hugely ambitious and expensive project driven by a sense of national pride after the defeat of Napoleon. The scale of the achievement is apparent on reaching the open section of Waterloo Place, where the drop to the Old Town is seen through triumphant arches. The bridge took seven years to build and almost bankrupted Edinburgh. George IV made a grand entrance into the city from Calton Hill on his State visit in 1822, and Regent Terrace and Royal Terrace were named to honour him.

Old Calton Burial Ground

GAOL AND GRAVEYARD

Back on Waterloo Place, on the left-hand side facing west towards Princes Street, is **St Andrew's House**, Thomas Tait's 1939 Scottish Office headquarters. It was built on the site of the Calton Jail, once Scotland's largest prison. Of this, only the mock medieval tower, known as the **Governor's House**, survives.

In the section that remains of the adjacent ★★ **Old Calton Burial Ground** ⑳ lie many of the great names of the Scottish Enlightenment, including David Hume, the philosopher. The obelisk, which was erected in 1844, commemorates Thomas Muir, the exiled revolutionary, and several other 18th-century political martyrs. George E. Bissell's 1893 ★ **Emancipation Monument**, depicting Abraham Lincoln with a slave kneeling at his feet, is in memory of the Scottish soldiers who died fighting in the American Civil War.

REGISTER HOUSE

At the east end of Princes Street, on the site of the old Theatre Royal, stands the former General Post Office building, the work of Robert Matheson. Opposite is ★ **Register House**, designed by Robert and James Adam, and in 1774 the first major public building to go up in the New Town. It is one of the earliest purpose-built public records offices in the UK and incorporates 100 vaulted rooms within thick stone walls to reduce fire risk. The building also contains a **Scottish family history centre**.

At the back are the headquarters of Scotland's ultimate heraldic and genealogical authority. The statue on the pavement in front depicts the Duke of Wellington on horseback. On the corner of North Bridge is the five-star **Balmoral Hotel**, built by Sir William Hamilton Beattie in 1902 and still the place to be seen enjoying afternoon tea.

Until 1799, Princes Street was largely residential. By 1846, however, a railway line had opened. Residents asked Sir William Playfair, whose hand is seen in almost every corner of the east end of Edinburgh, to mask the intruder with a wall and embankment. Today this space is the site of the multi-level **Princes Mall** ㉛ , a shopping centre which incorporates the tourist information centre.

Across Waverley Bridge, a statue of David Livingstone, the missionary and explorer, is set back in **East Princes Street Gardens**. Beyond is the figure of Adam Black, twice Lord Provost of Edinburgh and one-time member of parliament. Nearby is a statue of Professor John Wilson, who wrote popular articles under the pen-name of Christopher North.

The erection of the 200-ft (61-metre) **Scott Monument** ㉜ (open Apr–Sept: Mon–Sat 9am–6pm, Sun 10am–6pm; Oct–Mar: Mon–Sat: 9am–3pm, Sun: 10am–3pm) began in 1840, eight years after the death of the novelist Sir Walter Scott, one of Edinburgh's most famous citizens. Its suitable mix of Gothic fantasy and pure romanticism was the work of George Meikle Kemp, the winner of an open architectural competition for the work. Sadly, Kemp was never to see his creation completed: he drowned in the Union Canal while the construction work was still underway.

At the base of the monument is a statue of Sir Walter with Maida, his favourite staghound. The exterior stone incorporates more than 60 statuettes of characters from his books. A narrow, winding staircase of 287 steps can be climbed to see displays inside the monument and for views from the balconies.

Star Attraction
● **Old Calton Burial Ground**

*Below: view from Princes Street Gardens to Castle
Bottom: Princes Street and the Scott Monument*

Map on pages 18–19

5: The New Town

The Mound – Princes Street – Charlotte Square – St Andrew Square – Heriot Row – Queensferry Street – Palmerston Place

This route begins half-way along Princes Street, on the steps of the Royal Scottish Academy, and explores the Georgian New Town, including a stroll around the handsome residential area north of Queen Street.

Below: views to the Mound from Castle Street
Bottom: exhibits at the Royal Scottish Academy

ART ON THE MOUND

The Mound was built as a link path across the chasm between old and new Edinburgh, constructed of rubble dug out of the foundations of the New Town. By an Act of Parliament in 1816, the town council was authorised to build on it according to a plan agreed in consultation with a group of Princes Street residents, with a subsequent guarantee that gardens should be preserved as an open space, but it wasn't until 1830 that a proper road was constructed.

At the foot of the Mound stands the ★★ **Royal Scottish Academy** ㉝, erected in 1826 and surmounted by a statue of Queen Victoria by Sir John Steell. Behind this magnificent building is the no-less-splendid ★★★ **National Gallery of Scotland** ㉞ (open Mon–Sat 10am –5pm, Sun 2–5pm;

extended hours during Festival), which houses one of the best art collections in Europe. The Scottish collection is outstanding. Impressionism and Post-Impressionism are represented by some well-known works by Monet and Cézanne, and there are fine examples of many of the Old Masters, including Botticelli, Raphael, Titian and Rembrandt. The gallery's collection of Turner's watercolours is exhibited every January.

Both galleries were designed by William Playfair, in addition to the adjacent flight of steps which lead to the top of the Mound. In 1978, their name was changed from John Knox Way to the **Playfair Steps**. A new entrance to the complex, the Weston Link, leads directly from Princes Street Gardens, and connects both the National Gallery and the Royal Scottish Academy.

PRINCES STREET GARDENS

At the foot of the Mound, just inside the gardens on the other side of the road, is the world's oldest ★ **Floral Clock** ㉟, laid out annually with more than 20,000 plants; it has electrically driven hands. ★★ **Princes Street Gardens** were planted in the valley below the Castle Rock after the residents of **Princes Street** won their battle to preserve the view from their windows of the Old Town skyline. (This was before its properties were taken over by commercial concerns.) Developers were forced to give up their plans to build in the virgin space left after the Nor' Loch (*see box on page 50*) was drained. Although exceptions were later made for Waverley Station and the railway track that now dissects the gardens, and for the Scott Monument in the East Gardens, the view is unspoiled. Initially intended for the exclusive use of New Town residents, the manicured gardens are today open to all, and are well used by office workers and tourists on sunny days.

GARDEN MEMORIALS

Lining the gardens along the south side of Princes Street, named after the sons of George III, are

Star Attractions
- Royal Scottish Academy
- National Gallery of Scotland
- Princes Street Gardens

The Great Flitting
Before the New Town was built, from the 1760s onwards, the rising population of Edinburgh was confined within the cramped space around the Royal Mile, where tenements rose to 10 or 11 storeys, shared by rich and poor. After the New Town was established, the city's social stratification was, for the first time, reflected in its geographical division, as those who could afford to hauled their possessions across the Mound to this spacious northern suburb — which remains so different from old Edinburgh that it indeed seems like another town.

National Gallery of Scotland

Map on page 18–19

👁 The Nor' Loch

The loch was created in the 15th century as a defensive dammed moat, guarding against attack from the north. Through the years it degenerated into a disease-ridden dumping ground and at least 150 people drowned in it, many of them alleged witches, who were ducked to test their guilt, and suicides. The loch was contracted and drained by degrees from 1759, until the land was dry enough to plant with gardens in 1820.

St John's Episcopal Church, with St Cuthbert's Kirk on the right

various statues. Allan Ramsay, the poet, again by Steell, is first. Then there is Sir Frank Mears's memorial to the Royal Scots, who served, according to the legend, with Pontius Pilate's bodyguard in Scotland. Further along is Birnie Rhynd's equestrian statue paying tribute to yet another famous Scottish regiment, the Royal Scots Greys. The most recent memorial in these gardens is by Ian Hamilton Finlay, the 'concrete poet'; it commemorates Robert Louis Stevenson who, exiled for health reasons in the South Seas, yearned for the 'precipitous city' of his childhood.

The **Ross Open Air Theatre** (tel: 0131-228 8616) is a popular seasonal venue for concerts and dancing. It is especially well used during the Edinburgh Festival in August.

GARDEN CHURCHES

At the West End of Princes Street, on the corner with Lothian Road, is **St John's Episcopal Church** 🕉 (open Mon–Fri 8.30am–4.30pm, Sat 8.30am–noon; free; fair trade shop and restaurant in crypt), designed by William Burn in 1818 and partly modelled on St George's Chapel, Windsor. The interior celebrates the Gothic revival in Scotland and the stained-glass windows are spectacular.

Tucked away behind St John's, as Kings Stable Road curls round the Castle, **St Cuthbert's Kirk** (open 19 Apr–16 Sept: Mon–Sat 10am–4pm; free) is located in the gardens. The present church, said to occupy the site of an 8th-century monastery, was built in 1894. During the building, the foundations of six earlier churches were discovered. The present church has murals by John Duncan, and a fresco of St Cuthbert on Lindisfarne by Gerald Moira. In the kirkyard are the graves of Alexander Nasmyth, the painter George Meikle Kemp, the ill-fated designer of the Scott Monument, and Thomas de Quincey, author of *Confessions of an Opium Eater*.

Across Lothian Road is the **Caledonian Hilton Hotel** (with liveried doormen), built as a railway hotel rivalling the Balmoral, when there was a station at either end of Princes Street. Shandwick Place leads west towards Haymarket Station. At the far end are **Atholl Crescent** and **Coates Crescent**, with a statue of Britain's prime minister William Gladstone (1809–98).

CHARLOTTE SQUARE

The elegant New Town of Edinburgh is built on a grid system of broad streets, running in parallels. Charlotte Square, at the west end of the first phase of development, is linked by George Street, behind Princes Street, to St Andrew Square at the east end. ★★★ **Charlotte Square**, with a central garden featuring the equestrian **Albert Memorial** statue by Sir John Steell, is considered the finest square in the city, and is dominated by the domed St George's Church, today known as ★ **West Register House** and occupied by the Scottish Records Office. Designed by Robert Adam in 1791, the square is named after Queen Charlotte, the wife of George III, who was the mother of 15 children and died in 1818.

ADAM'S FINEST

Once entirely residential, the square is now also home to commercial concerns. The north side is considered Adam's greatest neo-classical urban

★

Star Attraction
● **Charlotte Square**

Below: New Town railings
Bottom: strolling in Charlotte Square

Map
on pages
18–19

Below: George Street statue
Bottom: the Georgian House

masterpiece, with No. 28, the headquarters of the **National Trust for Scotland**, containing a gallery of paintings by Scottish colourists and a fine collection of neo-classical furniture (open Mon–Sat 10am–5pm, Sun noon– 5pm; free), and No. 6, known as **Bute House**, the official residence of the First Minister of the Scottish Executive.

The three floors of No. 7, the ★★★ **Georgian House** ❸❼ (open daily; Apr–Oct: 10am–5pm, to 7pm in July and Aug; Mar and Nov: 11am–3pm) were formerly owned by the family of the Marquess of Bute. They have been refurbished by the National Trust for Scotland in the style of the late 18th-century. There is a fascinating array of china, silver, pictures and furniture, gadgets and utensils ranging from the decorative to the purely functional. Adjacent to the museum shop is an audio-visual room which describes the lives of the wealthy inhabitants of Edinburgh's New Town.

GEORGE STREET

The Georgian character of **George Street**, named after George III, remains relatively unspoiled. Traditional shops are interspersed with upmarket fashion stores and smart bars and restaurants. Statues, at intersections, honour famous men: Dr Thomas Chalmers, first principal of Free

Church College, at Castle Street; William Pitt, the British prime minister, at Frederick Street, and George IV at Hanover Street.

On the north side, between Frederick Street and Hanover Street, are the **Assembly Rooms** ❸⓿, originated by James Henderson in 1818, but later added to by William Burn, who with William Bryce added the **Music Hall** at the rear. With their magnificent crystal chandeliers, the Assembly Rooms have been the venue for many a great social occasion, and are now used as a Festival Fringe and occasional *ceilidh* venue (tel: 0131-220 4349).

At the east end of George Street is ★**St Andrew's** and **St George's Church** (open Mon–Fri 10am–3pm; free), built in 1781–83 to a competition-winning design by an amateur draughtsman, Captain Andrew Frazer of the Royal Engineers. Both the exterior and interior display a restrained elegance. A sign on the facade explains that this was the scene of the 1843 General Assembly of the Church of Scotland, from which 470 evangelical ministers walked out to set up the Free Church of Scotland. Opposite, a grander classical edifice, **The Dome**, was formerly a bank but is now a fashionable bar. Its extravagantly decorated 19th-century interior is also worth seeing.

ST ANDREW SQUARE

St Andrew Square, much altered by modern buildings in the latter half of the 20th century and the beginning of the 21st, retains a few of its original facades. The gardens at its centre are dominated by the 121-ft (37-metre) ★**Melville Monument**, a Doric column surmounted by a statue by Robert Forrest of Henry Dundas, 1st Viscount Melville who, as a key figure in Pitt the Younger's government, influenced Scottish politics to the extent that he became known as 'The Uncrowned King of Scotland'.

On the east side of the square, set back from the road, is the head office of the ★★**Royal Bank of Scotland** ❸⑨, originally the home of Melville's

Star Attraction
● Georgian House
● Royal Bank of Scotland

Shopping haven
Retail therapy extends from George Street and Princes Street into St Andrew Square itself. The London department store, Harvey Nichols, renowned for its designer fashion, has set up a branch here, and The Walk shopping arcade, linked with the St James Centre, provides new space for smaller outlets following the rebuilding of the adjoining bus station. Edinburgh's Jenners department store, which first opened in 1838, must these days compete with incomers.

Music Hall chandelier at the Assembly Rooms

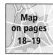

Map on pages 18–19

Driving tips
If exploring the Georgian New Town by car:
● Be prepared to drive on the ubiquitous cobbled streets.
● Make time allowances for 'going round in circles' — one-way streets abound due to civic attempts to calm the traffic.
● Expect to search and pay (meters operate Monday to Saturday) for parking. Always observe white lines marking 'residents only' spaces and other restrictions, as traffic wardens are strict and frequently impose fines.
● Walk or take a bus if possible.

kinsman, Sir Laurence Dundas, a wealthy member of parliament who reputedly gambled away his home in a game of poker, and later an Excise Office. Designed by William Chambers, the mansion was purchased by the bank in 1825 and refurbished with a magnificent domed banking hall which features on their bank notes. The equestrian statue to the front, by Thomas Campbell in 1834, depicts the 4th Earl of Hopetoun, a hero of the Napoleonic Wars and a governor of the bank. The grandiose Bank of Scotland next door is Victorian, dating from 1846.

SQUARES AND CRESCENTS

From the parallel routes of Princes Street, George Street and Queen Street, the New Town drops downhill towards Stockbridge, Comely Bank and Inverleith, encompassing the pattern of squares and crescents devised in James Craig's award-winning 18th-century plan. As seemed appropriate for a major Georgian city, north sloping streets were named after the reigning Hanovarian monarchy: **Frederick Street**, after George III's father, and **Hanover Street**, commemorating the six Hanovarian monarchs prior to the reign of Queen Victoria. **North** and **South St David Street** commemorate the patron saint of Wales, and St Andrew Square is named after the patron

Royal Bank of Scotland

saint of Scotland, crucified on a diagonal cross which was to inspire the white cross on a blue background of the Scottish Saltire flag.

PORTRAIT GALLERY

Queen Street, which runs parallel to George Street, was again named after George III's wife, Queen Charlotte. At the east end is the ★★★ **Scottish National Portrait Gallery** ❹ (open daily 10am–5pm, Thur until 7pm; extended hours during Edinburgh Festival; free). Housed in red sandstone Gothic splendour, the museum contains fine portraits of celebrated Scots including Robert Burns by Alexander Nasmyth, Robert Louis Stevenson by Count Nerlie, Mary Queen of Scots by Oeter Oudry, and more contemporary portraits such as Sir Steven Runciman, the historian, by Stephen Conroy.

Designed by R. Rowand Anderson in 1890, the building was a gift to the Scottish nation from J.R. Finlay, who owned *The Scotsman* newspaper. The magnificent restored murals on the front hall ceiling are by Phoebe Traquair. On the exterior is historical statuary by W. Birnie Rhynd.

TOWN HOUSES

Below Queen Street, to the north, are the town houses of **Northumberland Street** and **Great King Street** leading into **Drummond Place**, **Cumberland Street** and **Fettes Row**, largely designed by Robert Reid in 1802. In 1822, William Playfair added the two-winged **Royal Circus**. The substantial buildings of these sweeping architectural masterpieces were designed for Edinburgh's professional classes, with servants' quarters sometimes located at the end of streets and stable accommodation behind. Except for a few hotel developments and some offices, nearly all the town houses are now divided into flats.

All the streets off Queen Street reflect the period of their creation. **Abercromby Place**, designed by Robert Reid in 1805, overlooks

Star Attractions
● Scottish National
Portrait Gallery

Below: Scottish National Portrait Gallery
Bottom: Royal Circus

Map
on pages
18–19

Below: historic spot
Bottom: Moray Place

Queen Street Gardens and is named after Sir Ralph Abercrombie (1734–1801), hero of the Seven Years' War (1756–63). **Dundas Street** (now home to half a dozen private art galleries), which evolved from 1807, was named after Henry Dundas, 1st Viscount Melville (1742–1811), whose statue stands in St Andrew Square, and **Howe Street**, leading downhill towards Royal Circus, is named after Richard, 1st Earl Howe (1726–99), a celebrated admiral of the Seven Years' War.

HERIOT ROW

Built by Robert Reid in 1802, with additions by David Bryce in 1864, **Heriot Row** is named after George Heriot, who bankrolled James VI on his journey to London. In 1857, No. 17 became the home of Thomas Stevenson, father of the famous writer Robert Louis Stevenson, whose childhood memories here inspired *Treasure Island* (1881) and his poem, *Leerie the Lamplighter*. (The novelist also commentated on the decay into which some of the New Town had fallen in the late 19th century: 'It is as much a matter of course to decry the New Town as to exalt the Old; and the most celebrated authorities have picked out this quarter as the very emblem of what is condemned in architecture.')

Moray Place

One of Edinburgh's most prestigious residential addresses is **Moray Place** (car access from Gloucester Place on the north side), built on land once owned by Mary Queen of Scots' illegitimate brother, the Earl of Moray (1531–70). It has a 12-sided design by James Gillespie Graham. **Aisnlie Place** is named after the 10th Earl of Moray's second wife, Margaret Ainslie of Pilton. From above Ainslie Place, **Randolph Crescent** horse-shoes into Queensferry Street. Built in the 1820s, it comprises appealing arched doorways with Roman Doric pilasters, and is named after Sir Thomas Randolph (d. 1332), Robert the Bruce's nephew.

The West End

Queensferry Street initiates the first stage of the main road towards the former ferry, now bridge, crossing of the Firth of Forth. On the far side, the New Town extends down **Melville Street** and **Melville Crescent**, both designed by Robert Brown in 1814. At the centre of the crescent is a statue of Robert Dundas, 2nd Viscount Melville (1771–1851), by John Steell. The majority of the buildings in this area are commercial offices, although as you progress west to **Palmerston Place**, named after the 3rd Viscount Palmerston (1784–1865), the British Prime Minister, they become almost exclusively residential.

Fronting onto Palmerston Place and backing onto **Manor Place** is St Mary's Episcopal **Cathedral ④** (open daily 7.15am–6pm, 9pm during the summer months; free), the largest church built in Scotland since the Reformation. Designed by Sir George Gilbert Scott in 1879, it was funded by a legacy from Barbara and Mary Walker, two spinster ladies and the heiresses of Sir Patrick Walker (1777–1837), a wealthy advocate and landowner, who resided at nearby Easter Coates. The spires are a distinctive feature on the Edinburgh skyline, and the Walkers' original, small mansion house to the side of the cathedral houses the internationally-renowned **St Mary's Music School**.

> **Simple attractions**
> North of Queen Street there are no specially created 'visitor attractions' listed in tourist brochures; instead, the appeal is to fans of the superb residential architecture, with the added treat of glimpsing inside grand drawing rooms, often decorated in period style. Some of the basement courtyards contain tiny gardens, but the big, railed gardens, including those of Queen Street and Drummond Place, are unfortunately open to key-holding residents only.

St Mary's Episcopal Cathedral altar

Map below

6: Stockbridge and Dean

Stockbridge – St Bernard's Well – Dean Village – Scottish National Gallery of Modern Art

This is a pleasant stroll along the path beside the most interesting section of the **Water of Leith**. It starts at Stockbridge and proceeds upriver towards the Dean Village, ending with visits to two major art galleries.

Edinburgh's river is an attractive ribbon of silver and green which begins in the Pentland Hills to the southwest and snakes through the city to the Firth of Forth at Leith. In recent years the riverside walkway has been lovingly restored by the Water of Leith Conservation Trust, and fish and flora have returned.

STOCKBRIDGE

Stockbridge, named after the original footbridge spanning the river used by livestock, is a bustling shopping and residential centre to the northwest of the New Town. Stockbridge has become a district with character, also popular because it is within easy walking distance of Princes Street.

At the northern edge of Stockbridge, in an idyllic setting beside the river, is an 1860s housing development known as the ★ **Stockbridge Colonies** ㊷, comprising 11 rows of terraced houses designed for artisans serving the New Town. A particular feature of the gable ends of each block is the stone carvings of tools and implements belonging to different trades.

EDINBURGH ACADEMY

Extending east is Henderson Row which fronts on to the **Edinburgh Academy**, erected in 1824 by private subscription, to a design by William Burn, to provide education for the sons of the New Town (daughters were regarded as being less worthy of serious education). **St Stephen's Church**, which sprawls at the foot of Howe Street leading down from the New Town, was built by William Playfair in 1827. There is an unlikely tale that the bulk was intentional in order to hide the view of the pristine, neo-classical Edinburgh Academy from Princes Street.

Parallel with Henderson Row, adjoining North West Circus Place, is **St Stephen's Street**, filled with interesting curio and bric-a-brac shops.

ALONG THE WALKWAY

The present stone bridge was built in 1902, replacing the former bridge dating from 1786. From the bridge, on Deanhaugh Street, steps lead down to the ★★ **Water of Leith Walkway**, here known as the Deanhaugh Footpath, opened in 1981. Another access point to the Walkway is at the end of India Place. ★ **St Bernard's Well** ㊸ (viewing inside by arrangement with Edinburgh City Council), situated on the riverbank, is a small,

Star Attraction
● Water of Leith
   Walkway

Best in Britain
Stockbridge grew largely under the influence of Henry Raeburn, the great Scottish portrait painter. As part of a commercial housing development, from 1813 onwards, and as a birthday present for his wife, he built the elegant and leafy Ann Street (which, unusually, features front gardens), once described by the English poet Sir John Betjeman as 'the most attractive street in Britain'.

Stockbridge Colonies

Map on page 58

The Water of Leith

At Slateford, in the south-west of the city, the Water of Leith Conservation Trust has opened a Visitor Centre by the river (open Apr–Sept: daily 10am–4pm; Oct–Mar: Wed–Sun 10am–4pm). Exhibits not only trace the history of the Water of Leith's past industrial role and the use of dams, weirs and lades to harness its power, they also illustrate its natural history and the Trust's conservation work.

circular 'Roman temple', (designed by Alexander Naysmith in 1789) with a statue of Hygeia, the Greek goddess of health. Folklore has it that the spring was discovered by three schoolboys fishing in the river in 1760, and thereafter it became popular for the supposed healing powers of its mineral water. A plaque acknowledges the purchase and restoration of the well by Willimina Nelson, who bequeathed it to the city in 1888.

The pathway continues thereafter under the towering, four-arched ★★ **Dean Bridge** ④④, built by Thomas Telford in 1832, which rises 106ft (32 metres) above the river. For many years, until the parapets were raised in 1912, this was renowned as a favourite suicide spot.

Well Court ④⑤ is a surprising square of red Teutonic-style residential buildings, a Victorian experiment in community dwelling by the philanthropist J.R. Findlay, proprietor of *The Scotsman* newspaper. The clock tower, now an architect's office, was once the community hall.

St Bernard's Well, Water of Leith

DEAN VILLAGE

From Bell's Brae, a steep, narrow road leads from Queensferry Street and Dean Bridge above to the ★★ **Dean Village** ④⑥, taken from *dene* or *dean*, meaning 'deep valley'. Prior to the building of the Dean Bridge, travellers heading towards Queensferry would have had to descend Bell's Brae and cross the old bridge to climb up the steep far side of the gorge. The Water of Leith Walkway meanwhile skirts the base of the steep gorge, and passes the **Damhead Weir**, a rush of bubbling water which once powered many of the mills that were ranged along this stretch of the river.

Dean Village is around a corner, sunken into the hollow out of sight from the high town above. First granted to the canons of Holyrood in 1143, at one time the Baker's Guild operated 11 water mills here, manufacturing all the meal for Edinburgh and the surrounding villages. This industry went into rapid decline when larger, more modern mills opened in Leith during the 19th century. Similarly, the Dean Tannery, which once processed sheepskins, was demolished in 1973. In this picturesque hideaway, it is hard to recall that the bustle and traffic of the town is less than half a mile away. Secluded and hidden from view, there has been a considerable amount of residential, vernacular-style building in recent years.

Star Attractions
- **Dean Bridge**
- **Dean Village**

DEAN CEMETERY

From Dean Village, follow Hawthornbank Lane until you come to the footbridge over the ancient ford. Access to the **Dean Cemetery**, laid out in the grounds of the demolished Dean House in the Victorian era, is from Dean Path, and among the prominent Edinburgh citizens interred here are Lord Cockburn, W.H. Playfair, Sam Bough, the painter, David Octavius Hill, the photographer, and Dr Elsie Inglis, who founded the Scottish Women's Suffragette Movement. The cemetery is noted for its fine collection of sculptures and architectural monuments.

The 1887 **Belford Bridge** is the start of the Dean Bank section of the footpath, constructed on ground handed over to the city by the Dean Cemetery Trustees in 1975.

Out of sight, high on the left bank, is **Donaldson's College**. Designed by William Playfair in 1841, it became a school for the deaf in 1938. Queen Victoria is said to have remarked that it

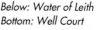

Below: Water of Leith
Bottom: Well Court

Map on page 58

Miller's hotel
On the bank of the river off Belford Road is the Menzies Belford Hotel (4 stars; tel 0131-332 2545), on a site where milling has taken place for more than 800 years. An explosion in 1971 destroyed the last of the two Bell's Mills, but the granary and miller's house survive.

Scottish National Gallery of Modern Art

was finer than any of her palaces in Scotland. On the far side of Belford Road is the ★★★ **Dean Gallery** (open daily 10am–5pm, closed 25–26 Dec and 1 Jan; free), built by Thomas Hamilton in 1833 as an Orphan Hospital. Today it is used to display the works of the Edinburgh-born sculptor and graphic artist, Sir Eduardo Paolozzi, and the National Galleries' Dada and Surrealist collections, as well as temporary exhibitions. Fabricated in Craigleith Stone, this imposing baroque-style building has a two-storey attic on top of the portico which features the clock of the old Netherbow.

Opposite is the ★★★ **Scottish National Gallery of Modern Art** ❹ (open daily 10am–5pm; also 1 Jan noon–5pm; closed 25–26 Dec; free), housed in a building originally designed in 1825 by William Burn for John Watson's Hospital and School, which merged with George Watson's College in 1975. Scotland's national collection of 20th-century paintings, sculptures, and graphics was founded in 1960 and located at Inverleith House in the Royal Botanic Gardens until 1984. It then moved here, and the Dean Gallery has provided additional space.

MAJOR ARTISTS

In the National Gallery there are works by major British, European and American 20th-century artists including Bonnard, Giacometti, Matisse, Picasso and Vuillard. Scottish art is strongly represented with Scottish Colourists, such as Peploe, Cadell and Hunter, and works by Robert Colquhoun, Joan Eardlie and John Bellany. The 12 acres (5 hectares) of grounds feature pieces of sculpture by Henry Moore, Barbara Hepworth and Jacob Epstein. There is a useful shop, and a pleasant, friendly café is situated within the building, opening out onto the rear terrace. The Dean Gallery also has a café.

Rejoining the Water of Leith Walkway, the path leads to Coltbridge and the Coltbridge Viaduct, which now carries a cycleway on the track of the former Balerno branch railway line.

7: Royal Botanic Garden

Inverleith Park – Royal Botanic Garden – Canonmills

This route begins at the West Gate of the Royal Botanic Garden, in Arboretum Place, where there is ample on-street car parking. Alternatively, Lothian bus services 23 and 27 from Hanover Street stop at the East Gate on Inverleith Row, near the historic Canonmills.

Map below

Star Attractions
● **Dean Gallery**
● **Scottish National Gallery of Modern Art**
● **Royal Botanic Garden**

EXOTIC PLANTS

A mile (1.5km) northwest of the city centre, the district of Inverleith is dominated by the imposing spire and bulk of **Fettes College**, designed by David Bryce in 1870 and founded as an independent school for boys, although it now admits girl pupils. Prime Minister Tony Blair was educated here. To the east is **Inverleith Park ⓸**, a popular area for football, tennis and cricket.

Adjoining the park, the ★★★ **Royal Botanic Garden** (open from 10am, closes Nov–Jan: 4pm, Feb and Oct: 5pm, Mar and Sept: 6pm, Apr–Aug: 7pm; free) is 70 acres (28 hectares) of superb landscaping. Exotic, beautiful and bizarre plants are found in this world-famous garden, which

Map on page 63

evolved from the Physic Gardens established near Holyrood Abbey in 1670, and which have been on their present site since 1820. An interest in plants' medicinal properties led to its founding by Sir Robert Sibbald, physician to Charles II and first Professor of Medicine at Edinburgh University, and Sir Andrew Balfour.

MAIN ATTRACTION

Beside the West Gate is an excellent shop, but do not be detained too long from the network of footpaths that lead on a journey of exploration. Attractions include the Rock Garden, Chinese and Woodland Gardens (with some of the finest rhododendrons in the UK), the Arboretum, and the ★★★ **Glasshouse Experience** (closes 45 minutes before the Garden). The orchid and palm houses are particularly spectacular.

👁 **Growing beauty**
There is a constant cycle of redeveloping, landscaping and replanting to rejuvenate parts of the Botanic Garden. Therefore, if you find one section of it closed, you may temper your disappointment with the thought that when you return it will be more beautiful than ever.

Arboretum Avenue was formerly the entrance to ★★ **Inverleith House** ㊾, a Georgian mansion house built for the Rocheid family, which stands at the centre of the gardens and hosts art exhibitions (tel: 0131-248 2983 for details and times). One of the best panoramic views of the city's skyline can be enjoyed from its back lawn.

The Terrace Café, next to Inverleith House, is licensed and serves a full range of meals.

Royal Botanical Gardens

CANONMILLS

To the southeast of the gardens is **Canonmills,** where the Canons of Holyrood Abbey, granted lands by David I in the 12th century, established a water mill on the Water of Leith. The writer Robert Louis Stevenson was born here, in Howard Place in 1850, and spent much of his childhood in the Inverleith area, before his parents moved to Heriot Row in the New Town. Stevenson used to go fishing on a nearby stretch of river.

The Water of Leith Walkway *(see also page 59)* may be picked up from the end of Warriston Crescent. The riverside path, Warriston Cycleway, follows the line to Leith Citadel Station, built by the North British Railway company in 1849.

8: Leith

Leith Links – Bernard Street – The Shore – Ocean Terminal

This route begins at the north end of Leith Walk, where Constitution Street leads into the town. It explores the historic area around the estuary and then proceeds west along the shore to Ocean Terminal. Leith is served by a number of buses running along Leith Walk from the city centre; No. 22 is a frequent bus to Ocean Terminal.

Map on page 66

Star Attractions
● **Glasshouse Experience**
● **Inverleith House**

TRADING PORT

Lying on the Firth of Forth, **Leith** is the port of Edinburgh. First recorded in 1143, it served as Scotland's foremost port from the 14th to the mid-19th centuries, trading with the Low Countries, France and the Baltic. In the 16th century it was twice almost destroyed by English attacks.

Leith was discrete from Edinburgh and in 1548, the Catholic Mary of Guise, Governor of Scotland during her daughter Mary Queen of Scots' infancy, made it her seat of government. When threatened by the anti-Catholic sentiments which led to the Reformation, she raised fortifications to defend the town. After her death two years later, these were pulled down by her triumphant Protestant opponents.

Below: local sign
Bottom: ship's restaurant on the shore

Map below

SHIPBUILDING

A century later the plague was to kill 2,000, almost two-thirds of the population, but by the start of the 18th century, Leith had established a major reputation for the building of timber vessels, and even Peter the Great of Russia paid a visit to learn about shipbuilding and, having done so, went home to create his own fleet in the Baltic.

In 1698 the ill-fated Darien Expedition set sail from Leith. A company had been set up in 1685 to trade with Africa and the Indies, with power to establish colonies. A combination of tropical disease and the hostility of the Spaniards, who had their own colonial aspirations, coupled with the refusal of Westminster to give assistance, led to the financial ruin of many Scottish families who had invested heavily in the project.

In 1720, Britain's first dry dock was built in Leith, and in 1779 Paul Jones, the Scottish-born American renegade, made an abortive attempt to capture the port with a small French squadron displaying American colours. Although activity boomed during the Napoleonic Wars, shipbuilding began to change in the 19th century with the introduction of iron hulls. Lacking the necessary deep-water facilities, Leith went rapidly into decline.

Incorporation with Edinburgh was forced on Leith in 1920, but the port and town retained a fierce individuality. Indeed, many old Leithers still do not consider themselves to be citizens of Edinburgh. Despite this feeling for tradition, a massive programme of renovation and urban redevelopment has taken place since the early 1980s. Once seen as a slightly sleazy port town, Leith is now home to young profession- als and media types. It's character began to alter and soon a slighly tongue-in cheek promotional slogan, 'Leith-sur-Mer', was unveiled. Fashion- able restaurants and up-market housing seem to be constantly sprouting amid the fine merchant buildings of a prosperous past.

And this new-found prosperity has strengthened links with Continent remain strong, that were forged as the wine trade developed. It was such a major business that, during the Napoleonic Wars, Edinburgh's City Council voted to ban the import of French claret, in order to 'bring France to its knees.'

HONOURABLE PATRONS

Tree-planting and wrought-iron work on the fine, wide **Leith Walk** give the approach to the port a suitably prosperous air, though the tone of the shops is more downmarket. At the foot of Leith Walk stands a statue of Queen Victoria, who arrived in her yacht, the *Royal George*, in 1842, but put ashore at Granton, along the coast.

To the right, Duke Street leads towards ★**Leith Links ㉚**, where the Honourable Company of Edinburgh Golfers established their first club- house in the late 18th century. Today, this august body is based at Muirfield on the East Lothian coast, but the 13 rules drawn up for the 1774 tour- nament form the basis of the game played today.

TRINITY HOUSE

At Kirkgate, accessed through the far end of the soulless shopping centre behind Queen Victo- ria, is **Trinity House** (tours by appointment, tel: 0131-554 3289). Built in 1816 for the Trinity Association of Mariners, which has occupied the site since 1555, the house has a magnificent inte- rior and contains many paintings, models and rare artefacts relating to Leith's maritime history.

The Kirkgate pedestrian walkway (with flats at the north end drawing attention to the contrast between living standards here and at the gentrified

> **Royal sport**
> Leith Links lays claim to an even longer history as a golf course than the venerable St Andrews, although it was originally common ground shared with grazing cattle, horse-riders and linen bleach- ers. James II banned golf on the links in 1457 because it interfered with archery practice, but 50 years later James IV took up the game himself, and Charles I was playing golf at Leith when news was brought to him of the Irish rebellion in 1642.

Leith Links

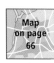

Map
on page
66

Ancient parish

The current South Leith Parish Church is largely Victorian, but it has been remodelled from the remains of a large 15th-century church, St Mary's, that was partly destroyed during the 1560 Siege of Leith by the Protestant adversaries of Mary of Guise. Stones in the kirkyard date back to this earlier age, remembering merchants, seamen and members of the trade guilds, who built chapels alongside the nave.

waterfront) replaced a once thriving street, lined with shops, pubs and a music hall, which was demolished in the 1960s. The name refers to **South Leith Parish Church**, which still stands opposite Trinity House (for access, including guided tours, tel: 0131-554 2578).

DOCKS APPROACH

Constitution Street continues northward from the foot of Leith Walk to the superb **Leith Assembly Rooms** �51 on the right, used mainly for private parties and functions. The road then approaches **Leith Docks**, evolved from John Rennie's plan in the early 19th century. The Victoria Docks were built in 1851; the Albert Docks in 1869, and the Edinburgh Docks in 1881.

The buildings of ★ **Bernard Street** �52, with the **Old Leith Bank** at its centre, mostly date from the 1770s. A statue of Robert Burns faces Constitution Street. **Bernard Street Bridge**, which crosses the river to Commercial Street, was originally a drawbridge dating from the early 19th century. It was rebuilt in the 1950s.

Leith Custom House

THE SHORE

Along ★★ **The Shore**, which hugs the east bank of the Water of Leith, and all around this area, are attractive bars and restaurants. The original **King's Wark**, now a cosy pub, was built by James I in 1438, but burnt down two centuries later. Since then it has been rebuilt and restored four times after successive fires. The former pleasure yacht *Ocean Mist*, which belonged to the Irish Guinness family, is now a restaurant and nightclub called Cruz

On the approach road to the docks is the **Signal Tower** �53, built in 1686, which once had a two-storey timber windmill on top of the existing tower. At the time of the Napoleonic Wars it was converted to enable flag communication with ships on the Firth of Forth. Beyond it, a pedestrian square has been laid in front of the stylish Malmaison Hotel, converted from the Victorian Seamen's Mission building.

Lamb's House ㊿, a 17th-century merchant's house in Water Street, was where Mary Queen of Scots allegedly rested upon her return to Scottish soil in 1561. It has been restored by the National Trust for Scotland and currently serves as a day centre for the elderly.

Across Bernard Street Bridge is the **Leith Custom House**. Designed by Robert Reid, it dates from 1812; it is currently owned by the National Museums of Scotland and is used for storage. King's Landing nearby was where George IV stepped ashore on his celebrated visit to Edinburgh in 1822.

Behind the warehouses converted into restaurants on Commercial Street are the headquarters of the **Scottish Executive**, purpose-built for its predecessor, the Scottish Office, in 1994.

WESTBOUND

To the west of Commercial Street are the Sands where pirates were hanged 'within the floddis mark'. The last such execution for piracy took place in 1823, when two foreigners expiated their crime on a gibbet erected opposite the foot of Constitution Street.

From Commercial Street, the coastal road runs alongside the shore of the Firth of Forth to the former fishing village of Newhaven, and

Star Attraction
● The Shore

Below: Lamb's House
Bottom: Newhaven

Map
on page
66

Whaling port

The first penguins to arrive at Edinburgh Zoo did so courtesy of the Leith-based whaling company, Christian Salveson & Co, which in 1908 set up a Leith Harbour on the bleak coastline of South Georgia in the Antarctic. By 1911 this was the biggest whaling company in the world. The Salvesons quit the business when the price of whale oil fell in the 1960s, but the zoo is still renowned for its penguins.

the popular yacht harbour at **Granton**, both undergoing major development, then onwards towards Cramond.

Newhaven was built by James IV in the 16th century as a dockyard for his expanding navy. He was determined to create the largest ocean-going vessel of his age, and thus the *Great Michael* was constructed here, 240ft (73 metres) long, to carry 300 sailors, 1,000 soldiers and 120 gunners.

BRITANNIA

Ocean Terminal and the ★★★ **Royal Yacht Britannia** ⑤ (open daily; Mar–Oct: 9.30am–4.30pm; Nov–Feb: 10am–3.30pm) are in the western docks. The Royal Yacht, launched in 1953, came to rest here in 1998 and the Terminal was built around it. A visitor centre introduces the 412-ft (125-metre) 'yacht', and the Royal Family's accommodation, and the 240-strong crew's quarters, give an insight into life at sea. An audio-guide has facts and anecdotes.

The glazed Ocean Terminal shopping and leisure centre (open Mon–Fri 10am–8pm, Sat 10am–7pm, Sun 11am–6pm), affords views over the Forth from its concourses and open-plan restaurants. The huge development was opened in 2001 and provides a great alternative for those who wish to avoid the bustle of the city centre.

Former Royal Yacht Britannia engine room

Excursion 1: Firth of Forth

Lauriston Castle – Cramond – South Queensferry – the Forth Bridges – Inchcolm Abbey – Hopetoun House (12 miles/19km)

This route is to the west of the city and begins by taking Queensferry Road at the west end of the city centre. It takes in a castle and country houses, and includes the possibility of a ferry trip to Inchcolm Island and abbey, with a chance to see puffins, seals and dolphins.

Map on pages 72–3

Star Attractions
- **Royal Yacht Britannia**
- **Cramond**

LAURISTON CASTLE

Turn off Queensferry Road at Davidson's Mains to see ★ **Lauriston Castle** (open Apr–Oct: daily except Fri, 11am–1pm and 2–5pm; Nov–Mar: Sat and Sun only, 2–4pm). This also incorporates a 16th-century tower once owned by the Napiers of Merchiston.

Various owners have since built on additions, and it is now held in trust by the city as a museum with a collection of Edwardian furniture and decorative art.

CRAMOND

Those familiar with Muriel Spark's 1961 novel *The Prime of Miss Jean Brodie* (or the 1969 film version starring Maggie Smith) will recall the picnics enjoyed by the strong-minded schoolmistress and her girls at ★★ **Cramond**. A lovingly restored, 18th-century village on the estuary of the River Almond on the Firth of Forth, it is reached by turning right off Queensferry Road, beyond Davidson's Mains, or continuing past Lauriston Castle.

The name Cramond originates from the Cumbric *Caer Amon* meaning 'Fort on the Almond'. Cramond was the site of a Roman harbour station. Excavations carried out in the 1960s indicate that it came under the control of Septimius Severus, Roman emperor from AD193 to 211. The remains of a Roman bathhouse were unearthed in the 1970s close to ★ **Cramond Kirk**; the current

Cramond Tower

Map below

cruciform church dates from 1656, but the site was probably used by the early Christians. A recent interesting find, displayed in the Museum of Scotland, is a stone carving of a lioness devouring her prey, which would have been buried with a wealthy Roman.

Stuffed
Cramond Tower must be the only 14th century building occupied by a taxidermist. George Jamieson bought the tower in 1978 and has restored it to its former (albeit slightly altered) glory. The ground floor is used as a gallery for paintings and taxidermy displays. Try www.scottish-taxidermy.co.uk

CRAMOND TOWER

Medieval Cramond came under the control of the bishops of Dunkeld who had their summer palace at **Cramond Tower**, a small, four-storey keep, restored during the 1980s. In 1680, the Inglis family began to build Cramond House, which was completed during the following centuries, in the process of which almost half the village was demolished.

In the 18th century, there were four iron mills along the River Almond, and the first commercially produced Scottish crude steel came from Cramond. Today the village has become a popular summer yachting resort with a lively social life. In keeping with this, ★ **Cramond Inn** is today a popular restaurant and bar.

Popular refreshment spot

ACROSS THE ALMOND

Since 1556 there has been a tiny ferry crossing to the **Dalmeny Estate** opposite (currently suspended during the rebuilding of the jetty – call 0131-331 1888 for the latest information). You can walk round to the estate instead, at the **Cramond Brig** upstream; this is where 'Jock' Howieson rescued from thieves 'the gudeman of Ballangeich', otherwise known as James V, who was in the habit of roaming around the countryside disguised as a traveller.

From Cramond village at low tide, it is possible to walk across the causeway to ★ **Cramond Island**, although it is essential to take note of the time of the incoming tide times if you wish to avoid being stranded.

EXCURSIONS

Map on pages 72–3

The Loony Dook
It has become a New Year's Day tradition in South Queensferry for a crazy band of men and women to parade, at noon, half-naked along the High Street and then plunge into the cold waters of the Forth. Crowds converge on the town from Edinburgh to watch the specta-cle and contribute to local charities.

DALMENY HOUSE

At the Barnton roundabout on the Queensferry Road, the A90 leads to the ★ **Forth Road Bridge**, a suspension bridge opened in 1964. Turn off towards South Queensferry, and the road leads past the gates of ★★ **Dalmeny House**, home of the earls of Rosebery (open July and Aug: Sun–Tues 2–5.30pm). Designed in 1815 by William Wilkins, an English architect, it was the first Tudor Gothic revival house in Scotland.

The Primrose family acquired the estate, and Barnbougle Castle, a Norman keep situated on the shores of the Firth of Forth, in 1662. The story goes that the 3rd Earl, when rising from dinner at Barnbougle, was bowled over by a large wave of water and decided at once to build a larger, safer residence. The 5th Earl, Lord Rosebery, who was British prime minister in 1894–95, married a Rothschild heiress, and many of the treasures on display at Dalmeny come from their home at Mentmore, in England, sold in 1977. These include colourful tapestries designed by Goya for the Spanish royal residences, a selection of fine French furniture and a Napoleon Room, which is filled with the 5th Earl's collection of memo-rabilia belonging to the Emperor.

Swimming the Forth

SOUTH QUEENSFERRY

The town of ★ **South Queensferry** crouches under the shadow of the ★★★ **Forth Railway Bridge**, completed in 1890, with a total length over water of 6,156ft (1,876 metres). It opened up the east coast rail line to Perth, Inverness and Aberdeen. The ★ **Queensferry Museum** (open Mon, Thur, Fri, Sat 10am–1pm, 2.15– 5pm; Sun noon–5pm; free) at 53 High Street tells the story of the place and its people. The town was origi-nally known as 'the Queen's Ferry' in honour of the saintly Queen Margaret, wife of Malcolm Canmore, who encouraged pilgrims in the 11th century to use the ferry crossing to visit the shrine of St Andrew in Fife by granting them free passage. The ★ **Hawes Inn**, which dates from 1683, was used by Robert Louis Stevenson in

Kidnapped to accommodate the fictional meeting between Uncle Ebenezer and the Captain of the brig *Covenant*.

ISLAND CRUISE

From the Hawes Pier, it is possible to take a cruise downriver on the ★ *Maid of the Forth* (Apr–Oct: weekends 2pm departures; July–Sept: several daily sailings; tel: 0131-331 5000 for details) to the island of **Inchcolm**, where you can visit the ruin of **St Colm's Abbey** (founded in 1123), which is mentioned in Shakespeare's *Macbeth*. Seals and dolphins, along with puffins, oyster catchers, cormorants and fulmars, may be seen.

HOPETOUN HOUSE

To the west of the town is ★★★ **Hopetoun House** (open daily; Apr–Sept: 10am–5.30pm, last entry 4.30pm), the historic family home of the earls and marquesses of Linlithgow. The first house was designed by Sir William Bruce and built between 1699 and 1702. In 1721, William Adam was engaged to enlarge the mansion. He added the magnificent facade, colonnades and state apartments, and after his death the work was continued by his sons John, Robert and James. Most of the original 18th-century furniture and wall

Star Attractions
- Dalmeny House
- Forth Railway Bridge
- Hopetoun House

Below: Hopetoun House
Bottom: Forth Railway Bridge

Map
on pages
72–3

coverings can still be seen, as well as opulent gilding and fine classical motifs.

The large, delightful grounds are full of rare specimen trees, and magnificent views of the Forth bridges can be enjoyed from the rooftop. Visitors can wander at leisure in the magnificent parkland and enjoy the woodland walks. There is a red deer park and nature trails.

A couple of miles further west is yet another stately home, the ★ **House of the Binns** (open June–Sept: daily except Fri, 2–5pm), which has been the home of the Dalyell family for over 350 years. General Tam Dalyell, or 'Bloody Tam', raised the Royal Scots Greys regiments here in 1681 to hunt down Covenanters *(see page 38)*. The house, part of which dates from the early 17th century, contains many family portraits and an interesting collection of porcelain.

FIFE

Beyond the immediate surrounds of Edinburgh there are, within easy reach by road or rail, historic villages and towns worth visiting across the Firth of Forth, in south Fife. Most notably, Dunfermline is the burial place of Robert the Bruce, and Culross, another royal burgh, is a small village with a number of 16th- and 17th-century sites restored and managed by the National Trust.

Below and bottom:
views of Culross

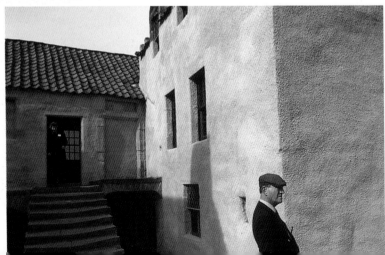

Excursion 2: East Lothian

Musselburgh – Gullane – North Berwick (21 miles/34km)

Map on pages 72–3

This is the longest excursion. It leaves the city on London Road, accessed from the east end of Princes Street, and enters East Lothian, largely following the coast to North Berwick. It passes through seaside towns and pretty villages and takes in a castle ruins, a magnificent country house and several interesting small museums.

PORTOBELLO

London Road leads past the 15,000-seat **Meadowbank Sports Stadium** erected for the 1970 Commonwealth Games. On the coast is **Portobello**, which reputedly was given its name by a seafarer who had taken part in the capture of Puerto Bello in Panama in 1739. It acquired burgh status on being amalgamated with Edinburgh in 1896, and by then it had become a popular residential and holiday resort. Sir Harry Lauder, the great music-hall star of the early 20th century, was born in a cottage here in 1870. In an attempt to restore Portobello's declining seaside appeal, large quantities of sand have been imported. The faded, old-fashioned seaside promenade has a certain charm and gracious houses offer desirable, cheaper living away from the city centre.

MUSSELBURGH

At the mouth of the River Esk, **★Musselburgh** was named after a bank of mussels in the 13th century. Its reputation as 'the Honest Toun' was earned when the inhabitants rejected a reward for honouring the body of the Earl of Moray, who died here in 1332. Flat and national hunt racing takes place regularly on **Musselburgh Racecourse** on the outskirts of the town as the road travels around the coast towards Prestonpans.

A hermitage and chapel dedicated to Our Lady of Loretto dates from the early 16th century, and

By train
A car is not needed to visit Musselburgh and North Berwick, as trains run along the east coast hourly from Waverley Station (first departure Mon–Fri 7.15am, Sat 7.37am, Sun 10.37am). The North British Railway first established this route in 1850, assuring the popularity of the seaside towns as day-trip and holiday destinations in the Victorian age.

Boats at Musselburgh

Map on page 72–3

was a place of pilgrimage for the sick. The name was taken by **Loretto School**, which has its grounds and houses within the town. One of these, **Pinkie House**, dates from the 16th century. Nearby is ★**Newhailes House** (Good Fri–Easter Mon and May–Sept: Thur–Mon noon–5pm; tel: 0131-653 5599), the home of Lord Hailes at the time of Dr Samuel Johnson's 1773 tour of Scotland. Built by James Smith in 1686 and added to in the early 1700s, it has a high-quality rococo interior, a fine library and landscaped grounds that retain their 18th-century design.

Adjoining ★**Inveresk** is a pretty village of garden dwellings, which has been conserved through the efforts of the Inveresk Preservation Society and the National Trust for Scotland. The latter owns ★★ **Inveresk Lodge Gardens** (open daily 10am–6pm or dusk), a delightful terraced garden with an attractive glasshouse.

LOCAL INDUSTRIES

On the coast road there are numerous small towns and pretty villages to explore. The first, **Prestonpans**, is not attractive but is historically interesting. In the 12th century monks from Newbattle Abbey started up a salt-panning industry here.

One and a half miles (2.5km) to the southwest is a former colliery site with 800 years of min-

Flag and flight

Situated between Haddington and North Berwick, it is worth seeking out the National Flag Heritage Centre (Athelstaneford, B1343; Apr–Oct: daily 9am–6pm; free) at the birthplace of Scotland's Saltire flag, and the Museum of Flight (East Fortune, B1377; 16 Mar–Oct: daily 10.30am–5pm; winter weekends 10am–4pm) in the hangars of a World War II airfield.

House in Inveresk

ing history, now turned into the **Prestongrange Museum** (open Apr–Oct: daily 11am–4pm; free). The highlight of the guided tour is the Cornish beam engine that pumped water out of the mine. The Visitor Centre contains exhibitions on various local industries.

East of the town, a cairn commemorates the Battle of Prestonpans, a famous Jacobite victory won by Prince Charles Edward Stuart in 1745 against General John Cope and his government troops. Nearby **Cockenzie**, formerly a thriving fishing village, is dominated by an electricity-generating station. Adjacent **Port Seton** is a family holiday resort with an attractive beach, camping facilities and safe bathing.

HADDINGTON

Further east and inland, just off the A1, is **Haddington**, once described as the 'metropolis' of East Lothian. It is still a bustling market town and the administrative centre of the region. A royal burgh from the reign of David I, it was constantly attacked by invading English armies. The magnificent collegiate church of ★★ **St Mary the Virgin**, away from the town centre overlooking the River Tyne, has been superbly restored and contains the medieval burial aisle of the Maitlands of Lethington *(see page 80)*. Believed to have been the birthplace of John Knox, Haddington was certainly the birthplace of Jane Welsh, the wife of Thomas Carlyle, the historian, writer and philosopher, and Samuel Smiles, the Victorian exponent of 'self-help'. The ★★ **Jane Welsh Carlyle Museum** (open Apr–Sept: Wed–Sat 2–5pm), in her childhood home, is beautifully restored to reflect her life and times. Jane Welsh's tomb is in another **St Mary's**, on Sidegate in the town centre (open May–Sept: Mon–Sat 11am–4pm, Sun 2–4.30pm).

Three miles (5km) to the south, on the B6368, is **Bolton**, a picturesque village notable for the church in which are buried the mother, sister and brother of Robert Burns. Gilbert Burns, Robert's brother, was factor to a nearby estate. Unlike his

Star Attractions
- Inveresk Lodge Gardens
- St Mary the Virgin
- Jane Welsh Carlyle Museum
- Newhailes House

Below: St Mary the Virgin, Haddington
Bottom: Port Seton

Map on pages 72–3

brother he was described as a man 'whose temperance and frugality were all that could be desired.'

LENNOXLOVE

Two miles (3km) away is ★★★ **Lennoxlove House** (open Easter–Oct: Wed, Thur, some Sat, Sun 2–4.30pm), formerly Lethington. It was the home of William Maitland, Mary Queen of Scots' secretary, and his descendant, the Duke of Lauderdale. In 1682, the house was sold to Charles Stewart, Duke of Richmond and Lennox, and the name-change to Lennoxlove commemorates Frances 'La Belle Stuart', the doctor's daughter who became a mistress of Charles II. To the annoyance of Charles, she eloped with and married the Duke.

When Lord Blantyre acquired the estate in the 18th century, it became Lennoxlove. It is now the home of the Duke of Hamilton and Brandon, housing many of the treasures from Hamilton Palace which was demolished in 1947. Among these are the death mask of Mary, Queen of Scots, and the silver casket in which she kept her letters.

Back on the A198 coastal route, pretty **Aberlady** was once the port of Haddington, but the bay became silted over. A mile onwards, a small trestle bridge over the Peffer Burn leads to **Aberlady Bay Nature Reserve**, notable for its colony of pink-footed geese. Sunbathers who wish to make use of the dunes of this wide, sandy beach should note that the west end may be closed off to protect nesting terns.

Nearby is the **Myreton Motor Museum** (open Easter–Oct: daily 10am–6pm; Nov–Easter: 10am–5pm), which accommodates vintage cars, commercial vehicles and bicycles.

> **Anglo-greens**
> In common with other East Lothian villages, Dirleton is more English than typically Scottish in its layout. The appealing grouping of houses around a 'green' is a feature which may have originated during the 7th-century expansion of Anglian Northumbria into southeast Scotland. Another good example is Gifford, on the B6370 south of Haddington, which epitomises the neat yet characterful prosperity of this agricultural region.

Lennoxlove House

GULLANE

Next stop is **Gullane**, a famous golfing village with three of its own 18-hole courses adjoining the Luffness course to the south. To the east is the championship course of **Muirfield**, an exclusive club that regularly hosts the Open Championship, the world's top golf tournament. The **Heritage of**

Golf Museum (viewing by arrangement, tel: 01875-870277), on West Links Road, tells the story of golf's development down the centuries. Gullane also has a wonderful long, sandy beach, offering walks by the dunes, either east to North Berwick or west to Aberlady.

Dirleton is an attractive village where houses, a 17th century church, and a hotel front onto a green across from the ruins of ★★ **Dirleton Castle** (open Apr–Sept: daily 9.30am–6.30pm; Oct–Mar: Mon–Sat 9.30am–4.30pm, Sun 2–4pm), built by the Norman de Vaux family in 1225. In the grounds is a 17th-century bowling green and a dovecote dating from the same period. In 1650, the castle was virtually destroyed by General Monk and his Commonwealth artillery, although the ruins are substantial and are surrounded by the world's longest herbaceous border.

NORTH BERWICK

The seaside town of ★ **North Berwick** sprang up on a promontory between two sheltered, sandy bays and prospered as a fishing port. It was incorporated as a royal burgh by Robert III, and is dominated by **North Berwick Law**, a mound rising to 613ft (187 metres) above sea level. On the summit can be seen the jaw bones of a whale. Today this pretty seaside town is a

Star Attractions
● Lennoxlove House
● Dirleton Castle

Below: North Berwick
Bottom: Dirleton Castle

Map
on pages
72–3

Below: Bass Rock
Bottom: Tantallon Castle

yachting and family holiday resort which relies mainly on tourism.

On the harbour, the **Scottish Seabird Centre** (open from 10am, closes: Apr–Oct, daily 6pm; Nov–Jan, Mon–Fri 4pm, Sat–Sun 5.30pm; Feb–Mar, Mon–Fri 5pm, Sat–Sun 5.30pm) has viewing platforms for watching birds on the offshore islands, an exhibition and video, and live film of gannets relayed from a remote camera on **Bass Rock**, which rises 312ft (95 metres) above the sea and supports a nesting colony. Half-way up the rock are the ruins of St Baldred's Chapel, named after an 8th-century hermit. Jacobite and other prisoners were held here, but today it is a bird sanctuary. Boat trips from North Berwick Harbour can be made to the bird islands.

TANTALLON CASTLE

East of the town, as the A198 turns south, headed for Dunbar, are the dramatic cliff-top ruins of 14th-century **Tantallon Castle** (open Apr–Sept: daily 9.30am–6.30pm; Oct–Mar: Mon–Wed and Sat 9.30am–4.30pm, Thur 9.30am–12.30pm, Sun 2–4.30pm), formidable fortress of the Douglas Family, one of the most powerful baronial families in Scotland. The walls are 14ft (4.3 metres) thick, and the well drops 100ft (30 metres) into rock. It was once considered the most impregnable castle in Scotland but has been in ruins for around 300 years.

Excursion 3: West

Corstorphine – Ingliston – Linlithgow – Falkirk (25 miles/40km)

This route runs due west of Edinburgh, past the zoo, to Linlithgow, with its Palace, birthplace of Mary Queen of Scots and then to Falkirk with its Wheel, a marvel of 21st-century engineering. At both Linlithgow and Falkirk there are opportunities for canal trips.

Map on pages 72–3

Star Attraction
• Edinburgh Zoo

MURRAYFIELD

At **Murrayfield**, off the A8, is the Scottish Rugby Union's international stadium, and the adjoining ice rink *(see page 110)* is popular with curling clubs. (This is one of Scotland's national sports, and the British Ladies Team, all Scots, won a gold medal at the 2002 Winter Olympics.) Further west, situated on 70 acres (28 hectares) of landscaped hillside is ★★**Edinburgh Zoo** (open daily Apr–Sept: 9am–6pm; Oct and Mar: 9am–5pm; Nov–Feb: 9am–4.30pm). The zoo, Britain's second largest, has a penguin parade every day at 2pm, April to September.

> **Steam railway**
> The A706 north from Linlithgow leads to Bo'ness, where an old station is the terminus of the Bo'ness & Kinneil steam railway. The 3-mile (5km) trip (open late Mar–Oct: weekends, and daily in July and Aug; trains depart 11am–3pm) begins or ends at Birkhill Fireclay Mine, where passengers can go on a guided walk through the beautiful Avon Gorge (tel: 01506 822298).

Corstorphine Sycamore

CORSTORPHINE

Corstorphine Hill, which rises 530ft (162 metres) above the zoo, features **Clermiston Tower**, built in 1871 to mark the centenary of Sir Walter Scott's birth. The village of **Corstorphine** has a 15th-century collegiate church with pre-Reformation tombs. In the village, there is a 17th-century circular dovecote, close to the 55-ft (17-metre) high **Corstorphine Sycamore**, a botanical sub-species. The 'White Lady of Corstorphine', said to be the ghostly mistress of a 17th-century local landowner, is sometimes seen to take a turn about the tree.

Continue westwards and immediately beyond Edinburgh airport, exit from the Newbridge roundabout on the M9 which, just after junction 1a, passes **Niddry Castle**. It was here in 1568 that Mary Queen of Scots fled, following her escape from imprisonment in Loch Leven castle.

Hamlet's Castle

On a promontory on the coast, just north of Linlithgow, stands Blackness Castle (open Apr–Sept: daily 9.30am–6.30pm; Oct–Mar: Sat–Wed 9.30am–4.30pm; last entry 30 minutes before close; closed 25–26 Dec and 1–2 Jan); it was built in the 15th century by Sir George Crichton, Earl of Caithness, a member of one of the most powerful families in Scotland. It's been used through the years as a state prison, garrison fortress and armaments depot. More recently however, the dramatically sited castle was a film location for *Hamlet*, starring Mel Gibson.

LINLITHGOW PALACE

A few miles on, exit from junction 3 and arrive at ★★★ **Linlithgow Palace** (open daily; 25 Mar–30 Sept: 9.30am–6.30pm; Oct–Mar: 9.30am–4.30pm; last entry 45 minutes before close; closed 25–26 Dec and 1–2 Jan), James I built a palace here in 1425. His grandson and great-grandson made additions, and James V was born here in 1512. In 1542 Mary, Queen of Scots was also born here, and the future Charles I was brought up at Linlithgow with his brother and sister, before his father inherited the throne of England and the family moved to London. Charles returned briefly to the palace in 1633, and Oliver Cromwell wintered here during his 1650 punitive trip to Scotland. After that the palace was largely abandoned until, almost a century after Cromwell's visit, it was set on fire following Prince Charles Edward Stuart's retreat from England. What remain are extensive, partially restored ruins.

ROYAL BURGH

Many of the buildings in the royal burgh of ★ **Linlithgow** have been restored by the National Trust for Scotland. **St Michael's Parish Church** (open Apr–Sept: daily 10am–4.30pm; Oct–Mar: Mon–Fri 10am–3pm; free), close to the palace and dating from the 15th century, is listed as one of the finest medieval churches in Scotland. Its 'crown of thorns'

Linlithgow Palace

Star Attractions
● Linlithgow Palace
● Linlithgow Canal Centre
● Falkirk Wheel

spire, however, is modern; it was lowered by heli-copter in 1964. Edward I of England used Linlith-gow as a base for his attack on Stirling, but the English garrison was taken by Scottish soldiers smuggled inside the walls in a hay waggon. Find out more at the local museum, **The Linlithgow Story** (open Easter–Oct: Mon– Sat 10am–5pm, Sun 1–4pm), which has a terraced garden with herbs and fruit trees, and a good view of the palace and church.

The ★★ **Linlithgow Canal Centre** (open Easter -mid-Oct: Sat and Sun 2–5pm; July and Aug: daily 2–5pm; free) houses records, photographs and relics relating to the Union Canal, correctly titled the Edin-burgh and Glasgow Canal, which officially closed in 1965. This canal connected with Lock 16 of the Forth and Clyde Canal at Falkirk, making it pos-sible to sail all the way from Edinburgh to Glasgow. Although commercial traffic no longer plies the canal, frequent short canal trips depart from the Cen-tre and on Saturdays and Sundays a boat leaves at 2pm for a 2½-hour trip to the spectacular **Avon Viaduct**, the longest in Scotland. On the last Sun-day of June, July and August, a boat departs at 9am for the Falkirk Wheel. A bus departs at 12.30pm to join the boat at the Falkirk Wheel for the journey back to Linlithgow.

Below: royal crests on (bottom) Linlithgow Palace

ENGINEERING WONDER

To reach the remarkable ★★★ **Falkirk Wheel**, the world's first rotating boatlift, drive westwards through Linlithgow and Falkirk for 10 miles (16km) on the A803. The lift, opened in 2003, links the Forth and Clyde and the Union canals. Roadworks had destroyed the locks and building them anew was not feasible. Board an excursion boat (daily; Apr–Oct: 10am–5pm, every ½ hour; Nov Mar: 10am–3pm, every hour; essential to book ahead, tel: 08700-500 208) on the Forth and Clyde Canal outside the excellent **Visitors Centre**. The boat soon enters the Wheel's lower gondola and in a mat-ter of minutes is raised to the top of the 135-ft (35-metre) Wheel. It then leaves the gondola, sails along a short aqueduct and enters into the upper (Union) canal. Return to Edinburgh on the M9.

Map
on pages
72–3

Excursion 4: South

Liberton – The Braid Hills – Rosslyn Chapel
(7 miles/11km)

This excursion heads south of Edinburgh on the A7 from North Bridge, taking in the Braid and Pentland Hills en route to the enchanting Rosslyn Chapel, with the option of diverting west to the Royal Observatory and Ski Centre or east to Craigmillar Castle.

LIBERTON

The southbound A7 travels through the university and residential districts collectively known as the **South Side** *(see page 38)*. To the southeast is **Liberton**, a 'village' on a hill with a fine parish church. The University of Edinburgh has its school of agriculture and departments of applied mathematics, engineering and genetics here, at the King's Buildings on West Mains Road. The village name may be a corruption of Lepertown, after a leper hospital that stood here.

   To the west, ★ **Blackford Hill** forms a 100-acre (40-hectare) country park along the Hermitage of Braid, an estate with a castellated mansion built in the 18th century. After it was bought by the city in 1889, a section was given over to a golf course and another to the ★★ **Royal Observatory**, an

Seven hills

Blackford and Braid Hills are among the 'seven hills' of Edinburgh', from which fireworks have been simultaneously launched at midnight on Hogmanay (31st December) in recent years. The others are the more centrally sited Castle Hill, Calton Hill, Arthur's Seat (the highest), Corstorphine Hill and West Craiglockhart Hill.

Liberton parish church

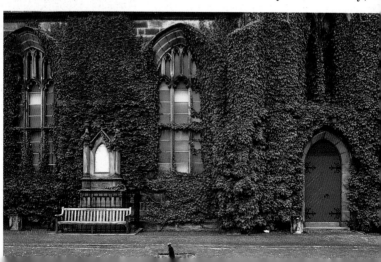

internationally recognised institution within the world of astronomical observation. The **Harrison Arch**, by Sydney Mitchell, honours a former Lord Provost of Edinburgh who secured public access to the hill. There are fine walks in the **Braid Hills**, which encroach on the Pentland Hills and reach across the city from Comiston to Liberton. Invading armies used to survey the city from this vantage point.

Star Attractions
- **Royal Observatory**
- **Craigmillar Castle**

CRAIGMILLAR CASTLE

On the east side of Liberton, reached via Peffermill Road (take the Niddry exit from Cameron Toll roundabout), is ★★ **Craigmillar Castle** (open 25 Mar–30 Sept: daily 9.30am–6.30pm; 1 Oct–24 Mar: Sat–Wed 9.30am–4.30pm; closed 25–26 Dec and 1–2 Jan). Sited between Liberton and Duddingston, this is one of Scotland's most impressive medieval ruins. The present L-plan tower dates from the late 15th century. Mary Queen of Scots fled here in 1566 after the murder of David Rizzio, her private secretary, at Holyroodhouse. Later that year, some Scottish noblemen are said to have met here to plot the murder of Lord Darnley, the Queen's husband.

Mary Queen of Scots

PENTLAND HILLS

On reaching the city by-pass from the A701, which skirts the east side of the Braid Hills, it is worth diverting west along the dual carriageway as far as the next junction (Lothianburn). A short distance to the south are the northern slopes of the **Pentland Hills** and the **Midlothian Ski Centre**, Europe's longest artificial ski slope (open daily year round; *see page 110*). At night, when the slope is lit up against the dark sky, it is said to resemble 'a stairway to God'.

Northwest of the Ski Centre, close to the by-pass but set in splendid isolation, is **Swanston**, a cluster of 17th-century whitewashed cottages. Here was a summer home of the Stevenson family, where Robert Louis conceived and wrote his early work.

Map
on pages
72–3

Mining Museum

The acclaimed Scottish Mining Museum (open daily 10am–5pm), on the A7 3 miles (5km) south of the city by-pass, is a fascinating and well-presented attraction. It includes a tour of the Lady Victoria Colliery (which closed as a working concern in 1981) led by former miners, and features a 'magic helmet' audio-guide and 'virtual' coal face. Newtongrange, where the museum is sited, is one of the best preserved Victorian mining villages in Scotland.

The Apprentice Pillar at Rosslyn Chapel

ROSLIN

Branching left to rejoin the A701 toward Penicuik, a left turn leads to **Roslin**, a former mining village on the banks of the River North Esk. The **Roslin Institute** research centre is where Dolly, the first cloned sheep, was created. Beyond the village are the beautiful woodlands of **Roslin Glen Country Park**, which provide the backdrop for **Rosslyn Castle**, built by Henry Sinclair, Earl of Orkney, in the 14th century. The castle drops down the cliff-face of a rocky promontory which loops around it on three sides. Extensions in the 15th century included a deep gorge cut across the access side and given a drawbridge, later replaced by a bridge. The castle, owned by the Earl of Rosslyn, a descendant of the Earls of Orkney, is partly converted into holiday homes managed by the Landmark Trust.

THE CHAPEL

★★★**Rosslyn Chapel** (open Mon–Sat 10am–5pm, Sun noon–4.45pm), also known as the Collegiate Church of St Michael, was constructed in 1447, a short distance from the castle. The interior is decorated with remarkable carvings, notably the elaborately carved columns decorated with flowers. The **Apprentice Pillar** is so called because it was carved by an apprentice stonemason while the master mason was absent. So jealous was the older man that he killed the apprentice with a mallet. There is a legend, recalled in Sir Walter Scott's *Marmion*, that Knights of the Templar Order, who fled to Scotland from Europe during the 12th-century reign of David I, are buried in full armour beneath the chapel. A more recent literary connection is that of the chapel's appearance in the book and film of *The Da Vinci Code*.

Back on the southbound A701 you are soon in **Penicuik**, where the ★ **Edinburgh Crystal Visitor Centre** (open daily 10am–5pm, Sun open 11am) provides a contrast to the rural pleasures of this excursion. Glass-blowing demonstrations, a shop selling exclusive lines and discontinued bargains, and a café are the attractions.

Excursion 5: Southwest

Morningside – Colinton – Balerno – Threipmuir Reservoir (10 miles/16km)

This excursion to the southwest of the city is a suburban and rural meander towards the Pentland Hills. It takes in fine homes in the well-heeled suburbs, country estates and tower houses passed down through generations of Scottish gentry, and the Water of Leith. Morningside is reached from the west end of Princes Street via Lothian Road and Bruntsfield Place.

Map on pages 72–3

Star Attraction
● Rosslyn Chapel

Below: 'Holy Corner' at Morningside
Bottom: Craighouse

MORNINGSIDE

One of the more popular residential districts of Edinburgh is **Morningside**, celebrated for its refined variation of the Scottish accent, much emulated by Scottish comics. Situated on the south side of the city, Morningside is fringed by the **Grange**, **Merchiston**, **Craiglockhart** and **Comiston**. Where Colinton Road meets the Burghmuirhead, which is known as 'Holy Corner', four churches, one on each corner, welcome you. On Colinton Road, **George Watson's College**, Scotland's largest co-educational establishment, was started with a legacy bequeathed to 'endow a hospital for the maintenance of sons and grandsons of decayed merchants'. **Craiglockhart,**

Map on pages 72–3

Hill walking
For the uninitiated, the best place to begin a walk in the Pentland Hills is the car park beside Flotterstone Inn and the Regional Park Information Centre, off the A702 on the east side of the hills. Here a board shows the many footpaths, and rangers will arrange guided walks and history tours (tel: 0131-445 3383). The highest point is Scald Law, which rises to 1,900ft (579 metres).

to the southwest, was evolved in the early 20th century as another residential dormitory of fine villas. **Craighouse**, whose bulk dominates the surroundings, was formerly a hospital, set up with the modern ideals of patient care in 1894, but now a campus of Napier University.

COLINTON TUNNEL

Further to the southwest, ★ **Colinton** began as a milling settlement neatly tucked into a sandstone gorge formed by the Water of Leith. For those following the more adventurous ★★ **Water of Leith Walkway** (see also page 59), **Colinton Tunnel** by-passes the village. It is dimly lit, but on the wall a drawing of a Balerno Pug, the small engine designed especially for the steep sided Colinton dell, can be discerned.

On reaching a stairway which leads to the footbridge, it is possible to take one of two routes. Following the old railway line, one path turns onto the north bank of the river and links up with the **Union Canal towpath** which goes northeast into Edinburgh. There's a pleasant riverside walk continuing out of the city on the south bank. Spylaw Park was the estate of Spylaw House, built in 1773 for mill-owner and snuff merchant James Gillespie, who was a great benefactor of social projects in Edinburgh.

The Balerno Pug in Colinton Tunnel

COLINTON

The first traces of a village at Colinton appeared in 1095, when a ford across the river was an important crossing point over the steep river valley. Colinton means 'village in the wood', and during the 18th and 19th centuries it was a centre for milling. On 28 November 1666 the Covenanting Army, which had risen up in defiance of Charles II's imposition of the Episcopalian religion on Scotland, was roundly defeated by General Tam Dalyell of the Binns at **Rullion Green**, not far away in the **Pentland Hills**. The **Covenanters' Monument** stands near Redford House in Colinton, now in the British army's Redford Barracks and Dreghorn Camp.

Colinton House, which has become **Merchiston Castle School**, was built by Thomas Harrison for Sir William Forbes of Pitsligo in 1806. A high road above the dell leads to **Bonington Tower**, on the Pentland slopes, once the home of Henry Cockburn, the great Scottish diarist. The road into the dell leads past fine mansion houses.

JUNIPER GREEN

On the far side of Colinton, the road connects with the A70 Lanark Road. **Juniper Green**, now submerged in a suburban sprawl, is a former grain, paper and snuff milling settlement on the Water of Leith. **Woodhall House** dates from the 16th century and the estate was purchased by Adam Cunyngham in 1629. At a later date, Charles I gave him the 'Supreme Commission to Punishing Receivers of Jesuits and Hearers of Mass'. Ironically, in 1961, the house was purchased by an English Jesuit Order.

Kinleith Mill was the largest mill on this section of the Water of Leith and produced 'featherweight paper' for export. The mill closed in 1966, and the area has been developed as **Kinleith Industrial Estate**. Moving on through the hamlet of Blinkbonny, created to house mill workers, the river passes through **Poet's Glen**, named after Robert Burns's friend and fellow poet James Thomson, who lived at the top of the glen.

Star Attraction
● **Water of Leith Walkway**

Below: Braid Hills foxglove
Bottom: sundial, Currie Kirk

Map on pages 72–3

Opposite: Malleny Garden
Below: view of Balerno
Bottom: Harlaw Reservoir

CURRIE

Currie takes its name from the Celtic *curagh* (a hollow) or the Roman *coria* (a meeting place). Certainly, there were Roman forts in the area. It is claimed that **Currie Bridge** is over 600 years old; it unites the two halves of the village. The present **Currie Kirk** dates from 1784 and has stones of the Knights Templar in its graveyard. The sundial in front of the kirk was designed by a village schoolmaster. Situated in the grounds of the privately-owned Lymphoy House is the 15th-century **Lennox Tower**, with walls 7ft (2 metres) thick. A legend suggests that underground passages link it with Colinton.

BALERNO

Balerno, whose centre is tucked below the A70, is on the highest workable stretch of the Water of Leith before it disappears into its source in the Pentland Hills. Its name is said to derive from *byrney* (a well sheltered place). The locality encourages the cultivation of local gardens such as the **Balerno High School Garden**, developed by residents and pupils.

There has been a house at Malleny, on the Bavelaw road by Bavelaw Burn, a tributary of the Water of Leith, since the 15th century. In the grounds of the present, early 17th-century mansion, ★★**Malleny Garden** (open daily 10am–6pm) is a delightful 3-acre (1.2-hectare) walled garden with 400-year-old yew trees and old-fashioned roses. There is also extensive woodland for a peaceful stroll.

Further along Bavelaw road, the turning leading to **Bavelaw Castle**, a 17th-century tower modernised by Sir Robert Lorimer, also leads to **Harlaw Reservoir** and **Threipmuir Reservoir**, popular venues for country walks. They are situated at the edge of the ★★★**Pentland Hills Regional Park**, which offers some of the most scenic hill-walking in easy reach of Edinburgh, and a rich variety of habitats for the wealth of wildlife to be found there. The highest point is Scald Law at 579 m (1,900 ft).

Architecture

One of the greatest achievements of the Scottish Enlightenment was the creation of Edinburgh's New Town, complementing the narrow wynds (alleys) of the medieval city. This architectural masterpiece was the result of a competition held in 1767 and won by 22-year-old James Craig.

Mid-18th century Edinburgh was a cramped, squalid place, quite unsuited to the ambitions of its citizens. It was hardly surprising, therefore, that George Drummond, six times Lord Provost, and his magistrates of Scotland's capital should decide to expand into 'the fields to the north', the land across the North Loch in front of the castle rock.

> **Old and New Town**
> Declared a UNESCO World Heritage Site in 1995, the centre of Edinburgh is a fascinating juxtaposition of medieval confusion and classical harmony. The Old Town is higgledy-piggledy, while in the New Town – now more than 200 years old – order and harmony prevail. The backbone of the Old Town is the Royal Mile, described by Daniel Defoe in the 1720s as 'perhaps the largest, longest and finest street of buildings... in the world'.

THE NEW TOWN

Craig came up with the solution, and within his grid system was created the largest and finest show-place of Georgian-style architecture next to Bath. Influenced by the Palladian architectural style, William Adam (1684–1748), and his sons Robert (1728–92) and James (1732–94), among others, began designing the classical squares and crescents of the first New Town, which evolved up to 1791. The second New Town was laid out to the north of the first, on the steep slope towards the Water of Leith, by Robert Reid (1774–1856). This concentrated on Great King Street, leading to Royal Circus, designed by William Playfair (1790–1857). Westwards, the Moray Estate, with the 12-sided Moray Place, was completed on an interlinking system by James Gillespie Graham (1776–1885).

PRESERVING THE CITY

The early 20th century produced little in Edinburgh that can be commended for architectural design, and the impatient desire for change prevalent after the end of World War II in 1945 caused civic vandalism to run rife. Following a plan of 1948, Princes Street was to be completely rebuilt

Opposite: Georgian houses on crescent in New Town
Below: overcrowded Libberton's Wynd

with a continuous covered walkway bridged at first-floor level. The concept was abandoned in 1978 – but not before much of the street had been redeveloped.

Happily, through the creation of preservation bodies such as the New Town Conservation Trust (now the Edinburgh World Heritage Trust) and the Cockburn Association (Edinburgh Civic Trust, founded in 1875), and a strict building policy adopted by the city authorities, both the New Town and the Old Town have remained mostly intact.

MODERN DESIGN

There are a number of recent additions to Edinburgh's architectural heritage of which its citizens can be justifiably proud. Many of these have managed to combine exciting modern elements with a need to preserve the city's history. Notably these include: the 1991 Saltire Court *(see page 9)*; the 1994 glass-fronted Edinburgh Festival Theatre *(see page 27)*; the 1995 Edinburgh International Conference Centre *(see page 33)*; and the 1998 Museum of Scotland *(see page 26)*. However pride of place goes to The Scottish Parliament by Enric Miralles *(see box left, and page 24)* which won the prestigious Stirling Prize in 2005 despite a series of delays and its hugely inflated costs.

Radical thinking

Enric Miralles, the Catalan architect who won the competition to design the Scottish Parliament, sadly died in 2000 before the completion of his design. Miralles' concept integrated modern design – such as roofs in the shape of upturned boats – with the historic setting of Holyrood, at the foot of the Royal Mile. After much political wrangling the building was finally completed in 2004 – at more than nine times the original estimate.

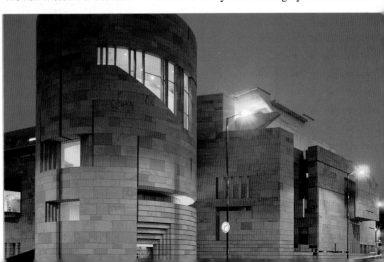

The new Museum of Scotland

Literature

Edinburgh has inspired more than its fair share of literary figures, whether they have been simply visitors such as Daniel Defoe, or native sons and daughters.

The Scottish poet Robert Fergusson (1750–74) didn't have much of a chance to enjoy fame. Employed as a commissary's clerk, he contributed to *Ruddiman's Weekly Magazine,* which brought him local success but little money, and he died insane and impoverished in 1774. Fourteen years later his admirer, Robert Burns, paid for a headstone to be placed on his grave in Canongate Churchyard, and on the same spot in 1987 the Saltire Society *(see page 22)* erected its own tribute to Scotland's three Roberts: Fergusson, Burns and Stevenson.

Bust of Robert Burns at the Writers' Museum

BURNS AND BOSWELL

Robert Burns (1759–96) arrived in Scotland's capital in 1786, aged 27. Having published the Kilmarnock edition of his poems, he was lionized overnight, but two years later abandoned 'Edina! Scotia's darling Seat!' for marriage to his childhood sweetheart, Jean Armour, and a farmhouse in Dumfries. His all too brief sojourn to the capital, however, had its impact and, apart from a monument at the foot of Calton Hill *(see page 30)* and a statue in Leith *(see page 45),* papers and relics are held in the Writers' Museum off the Royal Mile *(see page 22).*

James Boswell (1740–95) was born in Edinburgh, the son of Lord Auchinleck, a judge. A precocious youth, he ran away to London when he was 18 and struck up a friendship with the elder Dr Johnson, whom he idolised and later immortalised with the famous biography published in 1791. On his European travels, through sheer brazen charm, he succeeded in introducing himself to Voltaire and Rousseau. Returning to Edinburgh, he married his cousin, Margaret Montgomerie, and was admitted to the Faculty of Advocates in 1773. Apart from his *Life of*

Johnson, he is best remembered for his *Account of Corsica* and *The Journal of the Tour of the Hebrides*.

SIR WALTER SCOTT

There are two literary giants who will always be synonymous with Edinburgh. The first, of course, is Sir Walter Scott (1771–1832); the second, Robert Louis Stevenson (1850–94).

Below: Sir Walter Scott
Bottom: an artist's portrayal of Burns meeting the young Scott

Scott was born into middle-class Edinburgh, the son of a lawyer. As a teenager, he encountered Robert Burns in a New Town drawing room – a meeting of no significance to the celebrated bard but one which Scott would remember all his life. Following in his father's footsteps, Scott embarked on a career in the law which culminated in his becoming a sheriff (a judge in a local court). But, from an early age, writing was an obsession. Venturing into the deepest folds of the Scottish countryside, he recorded the stories and oral tradition of the people of the land, which he saved for posterity through his prose and poems. This was his great achievement. Throughout his life his literary output, often urgently undertaken to pay off his creditors, was prodigious. Late at night, passers-by outside his home at 39 Castle Street would notice the candle-lit shadow of a quill pen being wielded strenuously.

Scotland owes a great debt to the Wizard of the North, as Scott was known, because, had he not penned such masterpieces as *The Border Minstrelsy*, *Marmion*, *The Lady of the Lake*, *Waverley*, *The Bride of Lammermoor* and *Ivanhoe*, those old tales would have probably been lost forever.

It was Scott who encouraged his contemporary James Hogg (1770–1835) who, having tended sheep in his youth, became known as 'The Ettrick Shepherd'. Although essentially a poet, his prose work *Private Memoirs and Confessions of a Justified Sinner*, with Edinburgh as much of its setting, remains by any standard a remarkable achievement.

Thomas de Quincey (1785–1859), the English author of *Confessions of an Opium Eater*, was lured to Edinburgh by the literary scene in 1828 and he lived and worked there until his death in 1859. His remains are interred in St Cuthbert's Kirkyard, behind Lothian Road.

R.L. STEVENSON

Robert Louis Stevenson is buried in Samoa, where he died of tuberculosis. It had been a necessary exile, the Scottish climate being impossible for such an affliction, but he never lost his deep affection for Edinburgh. From his birthplace at Howard Place, the Stevensons, a prominent family of lighthouse builders, moved to 17 Heriot Row. At Edinburgh University Robert Louis studied engineering, then law, becoming an advocate in 1875. Thereafter he began to travel, selling his stories. In 1883, *Treasure Island*, inspired by the pond in the gardens in front of his childhood home, brought him fame. *Kidnapped* and *The Strange Case of Dr Jekyll and Mr Hyde* were both published in 1886, but it is in his poetry and letters that Edinburgh appears again and again.

Stevenson stipulated that he did not wish to have a monument erected in his memory. There are memorials to him in California, in Davos, Switzerland, where he visited, and in Samoa. In Princes Street Gardens, Ian Hamilton Finlay has created a child's garden where a flagstone carries his initials *(see page 33)*.

Literary lives
The Writers' Museum, on Lady Stair's Close just off the Royal Mile, houses portraits, relics and manuscripts of three of Scotland's greatest writers – Robert Burns, Sir Walter Scott and R.L. Stevenson. A short walk from here takes you to Deacon Brodie's Tavern, where you can learn about the eponymous character. Deacon Brodie was a respected councillor by day and a burglar by night, and is thought to be the inspiration behind Dr Jekyll and My Hyde.

R.L. Stevenson by Count Girolamo Nerli

Contemporary scene

There are a number of galleries in Edinburgh where it is possible to see contemporary art by local artists. Among these are the Doggerfisher Gallery (11 Gayfield Square, tel: 0131-558 7110) and Miracles (5 St Stephen Street, tel: 0131-225 2294). You might also want to check out the Edinburgh College of Art website, www.eca.ac.uk, which details the annual shows and forthcoming exhibitions.

INTO THE PRESENT

At Edinburgh University, Sir Arthur Conan Doyle (1859–1930), creator of the inscrutable literary detective Sherlock Holmes, was a contemporary of Stevenson. Born in 1859 in a now demolished tenement block near Picardy Place, he began a career as a medical practitioner in Southsea, but before long turned to writing for a living. A statue of Sherlock Holmes mourning his creator by Gerald Ogilvy Laing stands on Picardy Place *(see page 29)*.

Sir Compton Mackenzie (1883–1972), who wrote the classic *Whisky Galore* in 1947, moved to Edinburgh during the early 1960s and lived in Drummond Place. In the years before his death, he wrote his remarkable 10-volume autobiography entitled *My Life and Times*. Muriel Spark (b. 1918), best known for *The Prime of Miss Jean Brodie* (1961), set in the city, is Edinburgh-born.

Two contemporary authors who have concentrated on the darker side of Edinburgh life are crime writer Ian Rankin, and Irvine Welsh, whose novel about heroin addiction, *Trainspotting*, was made into a successful film.

The Talbot Rice Gallery

The Visual Arts

The fact that there are over 30 art galleries in central Edinburgh indicates the capital's status in the visual art world.

Following the genius of Allan Ramsay (1713–84), Sir Henry Raeburn (1756–1823) and Sir David Wilkie (1785–1841) in the 18th century, Edinburgh College of Art and the Royal Scottish Academy set about evolving a distinctive painterly tradition. This came into its own in the late 19th century with the impressionist seascapes of William McTaggart (1866–1925). During the early part of the 20th century, it was embraced by the Scottish colourists S.J. Peploe (1871–1935), Francis Cadell (1883–1937), and J.D. Fergusson (1874–1961).

More recently, Sir William MacTaggart Jnr (1903–83), Sir William Gillies (1898–1973), Anne Redpath (1895–1966), and Sir Robin Philipson (1916–1992) have added great integrity to Edinburgh's reputation for painting.

The four major city galleries are: the National Gallery of Scotland, off Princes Street on the Mound, the Scottish National Gallery of Modern Art and the Dean Gallery, both in Belford Road, and the Scottish National Portrait Gallery in Queen Street.

Music

Below: the Kirk of Greyfriars organ
Bottom: St Mary's Episcopal Choir

Edinburgh's high profile music-making revolves around the Festival *(see overleaf)*. This attracts many world-class performers in opera, chamber and symphonic music, and jazz and pop. However, it is possible to catch good performances throughout the rest of the year. Edinburgh is the centre of the Scottish traditional music scene, and many pubs and clubs across the city hold regular sessions. Check out the comprehensive website www.albafolk.co.uk for listings. Scotland also has a vibrant local jazz scene with many good local performers who regularly play in Edinburgh. A useful source of information is www.jazz-in-scotland.co.uk, which provides listings for events across the country. Although the city does not have a resident symphony orchestra, the Royal Scottish National Orchestra and the amateur Edinburgh Symphony Orchestra hold regular concerts. Scottish Opera and Scottish Ballet also make regular appearances.

Edinburgh's Festivals

The Edinburgh International Festival was created in the aftermath of adversity. In the closing months of World War II, Edinburgh's Lord Provost, Sir John Falconer, came up with the concept of a great celebration of the arts which would play a role in the healing process between nations. At the same time, he believed such an event would re-establish Edinburgh as a European city of culture with a worldwide reputation. Before long, a chance encounter with Rudolph Bing, administrator of the Glyndebourne Opera Festival and a refugee from Nazi Europe, proved the catalyst.

Below: Eddie Izzard at the Edinburgh Festival
Bottom: promoting the Fringe

Together they persuaded Edinburgh's naturally nervous city fathers – and more importantly a recently conceived British Arts Council – to put up the finance, and in August 1947 the curtain went up on the first Edinburgh Festival production. It was a resounding success and the word soon spread internationally that Edinburgh was the place to be – this despite Edinburgh's only licensed restaurant closing at 9pm at that time.

ATTRACTING THE STARS

In the years that followed, all the world's great orchestras began to arrive. Yehudi Menuhin, the famous violinist, became almost an annual fixture. Singers Joan Sutherland, Tito Gobbi, Elizabeth Schwarzkopf, Maria Callas and Placido Domingo came to perform, despite the absence of a respectable opera house. Margot Fonteyn and Rudolph Nureyev came to dance. The lack of performance space was addressed in 1994, when the old Empire Theatre was developed into the huge, new Edinburgh Festival Theatre *(see page 41)*.

THE FRINGE

As the main Festival grew, so did the unofficial Festival Fringe. Its programme now has around 600 companies spilling into every available performance space to present 1,300 shows in 15,000 performances. Its specialisms are experimental theatre and stand-up comedy.

Edinburgh has adapted accordingly, with successive municipal authorities taking an increasingly liberal attitude towards closing times. As a result, for at least four weeks of the year, Edinburgh can be said to be open all night.

SOMETHING FOR EVERYONE

Today several festivals take place concurrently during the month of August. There's the Edinburgh International Festival itself (tel: 0131-473 2001), the Edinburgh Festival Fringe (tel: 0131-226 0026), the Edinburgh Film Festival (tel: 0131-228 4051), the Edinburgh Military Tattoo (tel: 08707-555 118), the Edinburgh International Jazz and Blues Festival (tel: 0131-553 4000), and the Edinburgh International Book Festival (tel: 0131-624 5050). There is also a hugely popular winter festival that culminates in New Year celebrations, known in Scotland as Hogmanay. Edinburgh has always succeeded in presenting unique and unexpected events. The Edinburgh Festivals embrace all the arts, and the achievements and reputation of early festivals ensured that there has never been a shortage of world-class performers desperate to plunge themselves into the rich cultural pool.

> **Dropping names**
> The Fringe Festival is probably best known as the launching pad for virtually any famous comedian you care to mention. First there was Alan Bennett, Peter Cook, Dudley Moore and Jonathan Miller, who sealed their reputations as satirists in 1960. Then in the mid-80s Ben Elton, Rik Mayall and Adrian Edmondson came along. More recent names who have made it with the helping hand of Edinburgh are Ricky Gervais and Mark Little.

Fringe Sunday at Holyrood Park, for free festival events

FOOD AND DRINK

Edinburgh is a cosmopolitan city offering a vast range of international food, be it Japanese, Chinese, Italian or Indian, to name a few, but visitors will be well rewarded on sampling the best of native Scottish fare.

Scotland's fish and meat are among the best in the world, from North Sea fish and wild or farmed salmon to Aberdeen Angus beef (which escaped the worst of BSE) and venison and game birds from Highland estates. Cheeses from small regional producers are renowned. Alongside the variety of ethnic restaurants are a large number of establishments that concentrate on cooking and serving these wonderful ingredients, either in a traditional Scottish manner or with a modern, international accent.

Traditional Scottish comestibles of international renown include marmalade, oatcakes, shortbread and smoked salmon, as well as single-malt Scotch whisky; these high quality products can be readily purchased in Edinburgh, in both tourist outlets and superior grocers throughout the city, as elsewhere in the country. Other Scottish specialities are likely to be new to the visitor, and may not sound as delectable. Of these, the one most likely to be encountered by visitors is the national dish, haggis, consisting of lamb's heart, liver and lungs mixed with suet, oats and spices, boiled, traditionally, in the sheep's stomach lining. This is actually very tasty, but a vegetarian alternative is available! Generally eaten with mashed swede and potato ('neeps and tatties'), in upmarket restaurants haggis is sometimes incorporated into an entrée.

A cooked Scottish breakfast is a veritable feast, including not only the egg, bacon and sausage of all British breakfasts, but also porridge, Scottish-smoked kipper or haddock, and black pudding (another offal-based dish). That's how the day should start, and it should end with a nip of Scotch whisky or a pint of dark ale. In Edinburgh pubs try the Caledonian 70- or 80-shilling ale from the local brewery.

The delicatessans, fishmongers and cheese shops in Edinburgh hardly reflect Scotland's reputation for an unhealthy diet, with too much fat and sugar resulting in the highest incidence of heart disease in Europe. The abundance of top-quality fresh produce in the capital caters to the city's large, discerning middle class, who, unlike their poorer neighbours, eat very well. In recent years, organic produce has become popular and is widely available.

Restaurants

Most Edinburgh restaurants that serve Scottish cuisine have on their menus fresh Scottish fish and seafood, game, beef and lamb, often served with organic vegetables.

> **Food shops**
> Some of the best specialist food shops can be found on Broughton Street, Bruntsfield Place and Victoria Street. They include Crombies, 97 Broughton Street, with a huge variety of sausages, Something Fishy at No. 16a, and Real Foods at No. 37 for organic fruit and vegetables; Peckhams, a general grocer at 155 Bruntsfield Place. On Victoria Street there are farmhouse cheeses at Mellis Cheesemonger (30a), the Honey Shop is at 32a, and Cuttea Stark (26) stocks teas and coffees.

Opposite: the Royal Mile Pub

Around 30 of them are members of the Tourist Board's Taste of Scotland scheme, which means that they have been inspected and assessed as offering something special. Several are included in the list below.

Price categories indicate the average cost of a two-course evening meal for two: **£££** = over £50; **££** = £30–50; **£** = £15–30. Many restaurants serve less expensive *prix fixe* meals.

The Atrium, 10 Cambridge Street, tel: 0131-228 8882. Simple yet elegant food. Chef/proprietor Andrew Radford has won an international reputation in this post-modern style eatery attached to the Traverse Theatre. **£££**

Cosmo Restaurant, 58a North Castle Street, tel: 0131-226 6743. Italian restaurant established over 30 years ago. Popular for corporate entertaining because of intimate surroundings. Mussels cooked in their own juices with white wine and garlic are recommended. **££**

Creelers Bar Bistro & Restaurant, 3 Hunter Square, tel: 0131-220 4447. Fresh fish supplied from the Isle of Arran. Frequently changing menu. **££–£££**

David Bann Vegetarian Restaurant, 56–58 St Mary's Street, tel: 0131-556 5888. One of the best vegetarian restaurants in Scotland, in the heart of the Old Town. Stylish interior and an exciting international menu. **£–££**

Duck's at Le Marché Noir, 2–4 Eyre Place, 0131-558 1608. Innovative Scottish/French cuisine in the New Town. Extensive wine list, attentive service, crisp white linen and fresh flowers. **££–£££**

(fitz)Henry, 19 Shore Place, Leith, tel: 0131-555 6625. Fine dining, French brasserie style, with imaginative dishes, friendly service and superb wine list. **£££**

> **Take a break**
> Coffee Shops: Elephant House, 21 George IV Bridge; Café Florentin, 8 St Giles Street. Traditional tearooms: Clarinda's Tearoom, 69 Canongate; Kenningtons at Jenners, 48 Princes Street.

Henderson's Salad Table, 94 Hanover Street, tel: 0131-225 2131. Long-established self-service vegetarian diner with a changing menu and live music in the evenings. **£**

Howies, 29 Waterloo Place, 0131-556 5766, a fine Georgian building under Calton Hill; 10–14 Victoria Street, 0131-225 1721; 208 Bruntsfield Place, tel: 0131-221 1777. Very popular, locally-owned group of unpretentious bistros serving modern Scottish freshly prepared dishes. Branches have individual styles and different, regularly changing menus. Wine list or BYO. **£–££**

Iggs, 15 Jeffrey Street, tel: 0131-557 8184. Small family-run Spanish restaurant with an excellent reputation for wonderful food, including Scottish game and seafood. **£££**. **Barioja** next door at No 19 serves a lively selection of tapas.

Keepers, 13b Dundas Street, tel: 0131-556 5707. Intimate cellar restaurant offering high quality Scottish dishes at an affordable price. Closed Sunday and Monday. **££**

Kweilin, 19–21 Dundas Street, tel: 0131-557 1875. Large space serving authentic Cantonese dishes; perhaps the best Chinese in town. **££**

Martin's Restaurant, 70 Rose Street, North Lane, tel: 0131-225 3106. Central, but difficult to find tucked away in a lane off the Rose Street pedestrian precinct. Excellent game, fish and organic vegetable dishes, with Scottish and Irish farmhouse cheeses recommended. **£££**

Restaurant Martin Wishart 54 The Shore, Leith, tel: 0131-553 3557. One of Scotland's most highly-rated restaurants. Wishart produces the finest modern French cuisine using top quality Scottish ingredients. The seafood is legendary. **£££**

Oloroso 33 Castle Street, tel: 0131-226 7614. For the young and influential, this is the place to be seen – and to see from. Its fabulous location affords stunning view of the castle and the Firth of Forth. **£££**

The Pompadour Restaurant at the Caledonian Hilton Hotel, Princes Street, tel: 0131-222 8777. French-influenced dishes and elegant, Renaisance-style surrounding for formal dining. Try the finnan haddock cheesecake with caviar. **£££**

Prestonfield House Hotel, Prestonfield Road, tel: 0131-225 1333. Superb ambiance in 17th-century mansion below Salisbury Crags. Classic Scottish/ French cuisine. Outstanding wine cellar. **£££**

The Raj Restaurant, 89 Henderson Street, Leith, tel: 0131-553 3980. This spacious restaurant offers a waterfront view and Goan cuisine. **£–££**

Le Sept Restaurant, 5 Hunter Square, High Street, tel: 0131-225 5428. Long-established, friendly and informal French bistro. Excellent value. Daily changing fish menu. **££**

The Shore Bar and Restaurant, 3/4 The Shore, Leith, tel: 0131-553 5080. Very popular bar and one-room restaurant. Simple menu with a strong bias towards fish dishes. **££**

Skippers Bistro, 1a Dock Place, Leith, tel: 0131-554 1018. Brasserie-style with atmosphere. Specialises in fish dishes. There is a 14-page wine list. **££–£££**

Stac Polly, 29–33 Dublin Street, tel: 0131-556 2231, and 8–10 Grindlay Street, tel: 0131-229 5405. Modern and traditional Scottish cuisine in a tastefully themed Scottish setting. **££–£££**

Sukhothai, 23 Brougham Place, tel: 0131-229 1537. Authentic Thai cuisine, beautifully presented. **£–££**

The Tower Restaurant, Museum of Scotland, Chambers Street, tel: 0131-225 3003. Excellent, Scottish restaurant, sleek and contemporary, on the rooftop of the museum. **£££**

The Witchery by the Castle, Castlehill, Royal Mile, tel: 0131-225 5613. Atmospheric restaurant located next to the castle, featuring traditional/new-wave Scottish cuisine. Wonderful food and wine and a theatrical candlelit experience. **£££**

Pulling a pint

NIGHTLIFE

Edinburgh is transformed during the August festival, and bars and restaurants are granted special late licences. For the remainder of the year, nightlife is a little more docile, though many bars close at midnight or later, and clubs at about 3am. Details of current attractions can be found in local newspapers or in *The List* magazine.

BARS

New Town

The Abbotsford, 3 Rose Street, tel: 0131-225 5276. Round island bar and Victorian decor. Former haunt of Edinburgh's literati.

The Baillie, 2 St Stephen's Street, tel: 0131-225 4673. Cosy, spacious island bar with mixed clientele.

The Café Royal Circle Bar, 17 West Register Street, tel: 0131-556 1884. A fine, tiled bar which attracts a large and varied clientele.

Milne's, 35 Hanover Street, tel: 0131-225 6738. A vast, cavernous bar with a changing array of speciality ales.

Old Town

The Bow Bar, 80 West Bow, tel: 0131-226 7667. Twelve real ales and 135 malts – a connoisseur's heaven.

Deacon Brodie's Tavern, 435 Lawnmarket, tel: 0131-225 6531. A traditional Old Town Scottish bar.

Greyfriar's Bobby Bar, 34 Candlemaker Row, tel: 0131-225 8328. A student favourite, conveniently close to the Museum of Scotland.

Around Town

Bennets, 8 Leven Street, tel: 0131-229 5143. A traditional bar near the King's Theatre, with over 100 malt whiskies.

King's Wark, 36 The Shore, tel: 0131-554 9260. Cosy relaxed pub with a long history, at the heart of the buzzing port district.

NIGHTCLUBS

The Citrus Club, 38–40 Grindlay Street, tel: 0131-622 7086. Thursday to Saturday. Popular with students.

Club Mercado, 36–39 Market Street, tel: 0131-226 4224. Trendy, with wrought iron decor. Glam club events.

The Establishment, 3 Semple Street, tel: 0131-229 7733. A lounge-bar-style club in the West End.

Negotiants, 45–47 Lothian Street, tel: 0131-225 6313. Café-bar with a basement nightclub. Good food.

The Subway, 69 Cowgate, tel: 0131-225 6766. Young, vibrant and rowdy.

JAZZ AND FOLK

Bars with regular jazz residencies include: **Henry's Jazz Cellar**, 8 Morrison Street (Wed–Sun, tel: 0131-467 5200) and the **Malt Shovel**, 11–15 Cockburn Street (Tues; tel: 0131-225 6843).

Folk residencies are at the **Sandy Bells**, Forrest Road (best to telephone: 0131-225 2751) and the **Royal Oak**, Infirmary Street (nightly 10pm–2am, also Sat and Sun afternoons; tel: 0131-557 2976).

Ceilidhs

A number of places throughout the city hosts fun, informal ceilidhs – usually at the weekend. With their traditional Scottish dances, and often accompanied by live music (accordians abound in ceilidh bands), they appeal to a wide cross-range of locals and visitors of all ages. There is always an experienced caller to ensure that all the dancers keep in step during the energetic reels.

SHOPPING

THE OLD TOWN

The Grassmarket has some interesting small shops wedged between the restaurants and bars, and the area adjoining Victoria Street offers a wide range of curio shopping, with the Byzantium Market at the top featuring antiques and bric-a-brac stalls. **The Royal Mile** is mostly given over to souvenirs and tartan, but running off it is **Cockburn Street** for alternative fashion and a further selection of tourist kitsch.

THE NEW TOWN

Princes Street remains Edinburgh's main shopping street, with the predictable presence of the ubiquitous high street shops. Jenners was the only independently-owned Princes Street department store until recently when it was bought by House of Fraser. A few steps north in St Andrew Square stands Harvey Nichols while, around the corner, John Lewis is the anchor tenant in St James Centre. Parallel to Princes Street, pedestrianised **Rose Street**, **George Street** and **Thistle Street** provide a range of smaller shops, George Street being good for upmarket fashion. **Stockbridge** and **Broughton Street** are good for antique hunters.

OUT OF CENTRE

The **Ocean Terminal Shopping Centre** *(see page 70)* opened on Leith waterfront in 2001. Other complexes outside the city centre are the **South Gyle** shopping centre, **Fort Kinnaird and Cameron Toll**.

SPECIALIST STORES
Haggis

Crombies of Edinburgh, 97 Broughton Street.
Jenners, 48 Princes Street and Edinburgh airport.

Scotch whisky shops

Cadenhead Whisky Shop, 172 Canongate.
Royal Mile Whiskies, 379–381 High Street.
The Whisky Shop, Princes Mall.

Highland dress and tartan

Geoffrey (Tailor) Kiltmakers, 57–59 High Street and 555 Castlehill.
Hector Russell Kiltmaker, 95 Princes Street, 137–141 High Street, and 509 Lawnmarket.
Hugh Macpherson (Scotland), 17 West Maitland Street.
Kinloch Anderson, Commercial Street/ Dock Street, Leith, are kiltmakers to the Royal Family.
Stewart, Christie, 63 Queen Street.

Scottish designer woollens

Belinda Robertson Cashmere, 22 Palmerston Place; 13a Dundas Street.
Bill Baber Knitwear Design, 66 Grassmarket.
Number Two, 2 St Stephen Place.

Scottish jewellery

Alison & Roy Murray, 20 Thistle Street.
Clarksons of Edinburgh, 87 West Bow.
Hamilton & Inches, 87 George Street.
Joseph Bonnar, 72 Thistle Street.
Mappin & Webb, 88 George Street.

Books and coffee
Several large bookshops open late (until 8pm or later) and on Sundays. Waterstone's is at 83 George Street and 128 Princes Street, with Starbucks coffee outlets, and 13–14 Princes Street, while Ottokar's with a Costa coffee shop is at 59 George Street. James Thin, a locally owned company, has a big, mainly academic bookshop at 53 South Bridge. All bookshops have Scotland and Edinburgh sections of interest to the visitor.

ACTIVE PURSUITS

FISHING

There are a number of well-stocked rivers and reservoirs within easy reach of the city, and brown trout are to be found in the Water of Leith (season is from April to September; permit required). Sea angling on the Firth of Forth can be done.

Fishing tackle shops, such as Dickson & MacNaughton at 21 Frederick Street, will advise on regulations, places to fish and techniques.

On your bike

Cycling is an excellent way to explore the leafy Edinburgh suburbs and parks, and the countryside nearby. In parts of the city there are cycle lanes thanks to campaign groups such as Spokes (tel: 0131-313 2114, www.spokes.org.uk), who publish a map of Edinburgh cycle paths, available from many cycle shops and bookshops. For cycle hire, see page 113.

GOLF

Golf is thought to have originated in Scotland, so it is not surprising that the capital city is well provided with courses. Over 60 golf courses are within one hour's drive of Edinburgh, including Muirfield, Gullane, North Berwick and Dunbar. An Edinburgh and Lothians Golf Pass (7-day) can be purchased from the tourist information centre above Princes Mall, or on-line at www.edinburgh.org This gives discounted access to 20 courses, of which five are in the immediate city environs.

Municipal courses (open to all) are at Braid Hills (tel: 0131-447 6666), Carrick Knowe (tel: 0131-337 1096), Craigentinny (tel: 0131-554 7501), Portobello (nine holes; tel: 0131-669 4361) and Silverknowes (tel: 0131-336 3843). Contact Edinburgh Leisure (tel: 0131-650 1001) or www.edinburgh leisure.co.uk for further information.

RIDING

In Edinburgh itself, Tower Farm Riding Stables, at 85 Liberton Drive by the Braid Hills, tel: 0131-664 3375, are approved by the British Horse Society and offer tuition and hacking. A couple of miles beyond the city by-pass, lessons, hacking and pony trekking are also offered by Edinburgh & Lasswade Riding Centre, Kevock Road, Lasswade, tel: 0131-663 7676.

SKATING

Murrayfield Ice Rink is a popular venue for skaters throughout the year. Skates can be hired. Sessions in the afternoons, evenings and at weekends. For further information, tel: 0131-337 6933.

SPORTS CENTRES

Edinburgh Leisure manages the city's numerous sports facilities; call 0131-650 1001 or try www.edinburghleisure.co.uk for a full listing. Below are a selection of some of the best – booking is recommended.

Craiglockhart Tennis and Sports Centre, 177 Colinton Road, tel: 0131-443 0101. Indoor and outdoor tennis, squash, badminton, fitness classes, kids' courses and bouncy castle.

Jack Kane Sports Centre, 208 Niddrie Mains Road, tel: 0131-669 0404. Games halls, fitness room and football pitches.

Meadowbank Sports Centre, 139 London Road, tel: 0131-661 5351. Athletics track, all-weather pitches and squash.

Royal Commonwealth Pool, Dalkeith Road, tel: 0131-667 7211. With an excellent pool, but also a gym, sauna and soft play for kids.

WATER SPORTS

Port Edgar Marina and Sailing School, South Queensferry, tel: 0131-331 3330, offers courses in wind-surfing, sailing, kayaking and canoeing. Try also the RYA Scotland, Caledonia House, South Gyle, Edinburgh, tel: 0131-317 7388.

SKIING

The Midlothian Ski Centre is situated at Hillend on the Biggar Road, half an hour by bus or car from the city centre. Features include Europe's longest artificial ski slope, a triple lift system, an alpine lodge and restaurant, skiing and snowboarding tuition and equipment hire. Open Sept–Apr: Mon–Sat 9.30am–9pm, Sun 9.30am–7pm; May–Aug: Mon–Fri 9.30am–9pm, Sat–Sun 9.30am–7pm. Tel: 0131-445 4433.

HILL WALKING

The Pentland Hills *(see pages 90 and 92)*, which rise steeply from the southern fringes of Edinburgh (near Penicuik), provide some delightful hill walking, with splendid views constantly changing with the seasons. For information on the Pentland Hills Regional Park, tel: 0131-445 3383.

For guided hill walking and hiking tours, or if you want to go further afield, into the Scottish Highlands, contact www.walkaboutscotland.com

> **Safety in the hills**
> Before you set off, always tell someone where you are going, and what time you expect to be back, even if you are in a group. Take appropriate equipment and clothing with you – the weather can change very rapidly in Scotland, and can endanger even the most experienced of climbers.

SWIMMING

Edinburgh has a superb swimming complex built for the 1970 Commonwealth Games, the 50-metre Royal Commonwealth Pool on Dalkeith Road, tel: 0131-667 7211. The City of Edinburgh Council has Victorian swim centres, among which are Dalry (29 Caledonian Crescent, tel: 0131-313 3964), Glenogle in Stockbridge (Glenogle Road tel: 0131-343 6376), Warrender (Thirlestane Road, tel: 0131-447 0052), Portobello (57 The Promenade, tel: 0131-669 6888), recently refurbished and offering authentic Turkish baths, and Leith Victoria (Junction Place, tel: 0131-555 4728). Also in Leith is a leisure pool with flumes which is ideal for children; Leith Waterworld (377 Easter Road, tel: 0131-555 6000 for opening hours).

The Pentland Hills

PRACTICAL INFORMATION

Getting There

BY CAR

Edinburgh is approached from the south by the A1 coastal road from Berwick Upon Tweed, the A68 from Jedburgh, and the A7 from Selkirk. There is no motorway route into the southeast of Scotland, but this is compensated for by the beauty of the countryside.

The M6, which travels up the west coast of England, meets with the A74 north of Carlisle, which becomes the M74 and connects with the M8 northeast of Glasgow. Travelling east, the M8 meets with the Edinburgh City bypass, west of Edinburgh. The M8 also connects with the M9 from Stirling at the Newbridge Roundabout, northwest of the city.

From Perth, the M90 turns into the A90 before crossing the Forth Road Bridge and entering the city suburbs at Barnton.

BY COACH

There are daily and overnight long-distance bus services to St Andrew Square from London and elsewhere in the UK. For details, contact: National Express, tel: 08705-80 8080 (from the UK or abroad), or Scottish Citylink, tel: 08705-505050.

BY TRAIN

Edinburgh Waverley and Edinburgh Haymarket stations service incoming trains. For current fares and timetables, and also for credit card sales and reservations, tel: 0845-748 4950.

GNER InterCity operate regular hourly services between London Kings Cross and Edinburgh Waverley, 6am–7pm. The service, which takes around 5 hours, is popular and reservations are recommended.

The Freedom of Scotland Travel Pass from ScotRail gives unlimited travel on Scotland's rail network for 8 or 15 consecutive days.

BY AIR

Edinburgh Airport, west of the city on the Glasgow Road, is served by regular flights from London Heathrow, London Gatwick, London Stansted, London Luton, Birmingham, East Midlands, Leeds/Bradford, Cardiff, Belfast, Dublin and several cities – Brussels, Cologne, Copenhagen, Frankfurt, Paris, Prague, Stockholm – on the European continent. (Scheduled flights from North America – Chicago, New York, Toronto – and from Iceland land at Prestwick and Glasgow). Airport information: tel: 0870-040 0007.

BY SEA

Superfast Ferries operate car ferries between Zeebrugge in Belgium, and Rosyth, which is 30 minutes from Edinburgh, with a journey time of 17hr 30min. Information and bookings, tel: 0870-234 0870, www.superfast.com

Getting Around

Public transport information is available by calling free-phone Traveline, tel: 0870-608 2608.

CAR & BIKE RENTAL

This is well worth doing if you want to explore the surrounding districts and countryside. Car firms include:
Arnold Clark, tel: 0131-657 9120, 0131-458 1501 (airport).
Avis, 0870-153 9103, 0131-344 3900 (airport).
Condor Self Drive, tel: 0131-229 6333, 0131-554 8000.
Hertz, tel: 0870-846 0013, 0870-846 0009.

National Car Rental, tel: 0131-337 8686, 0870-191 0553 (airport).

Bicycles can be hired from:
Bike Trax, Lochrin Place, Tollcross, tel: 0131-228 6633; www.biketrax.co.uk
Cycle Scotland, 29 Blackfriars Street, tel: 0131-556 5560; www.cyclescotland.co.uk
Edinburgh Bicycle Co-op, 8 Alvanley Terrace, Whitehouse Loan, tel: 0131-228 3565.

BUSES

The two main bus companies are Lothian Buses (red/white/orange check livery with older buses in maroon and white) and Edinburgh First (large F in a pink circle). You buy a ticket as you enter the bus (exact change required); do not lose it before you reach your destination as an inspector may want to see it. For details: Lothian Buses, Ticket Centre, Waverley Bridge, tel: 0131-555 6363; Edinburgh First, tel: 0870-872 7271. Timetables, fares and route information are posted at the main bus stops.

TRAINS

Trains to and from Glasgow run on the hour and every 15 minutes between 7am–7pm, otherwise every hour and half hour going to Haymarket and Waverley stations. The journey time is 50 minutes. National rail enquiries, tel: 0845-748 4950.

TAXIS

Taxi ranks are located throughout the city centre, notably outside Waverley and Haymarket Stations, the Caledonian Hotel at the West End of Princes Street, and beside the Playhouse Theatre at the top of Leith Walk. Edinburgh's black cabs operate 24 hours. Taxi firms include: Central Radio Taxis, tel: 0131-229 2468; City Cabs, tel: 0131-228 1211; Radiocabs, tel: 0131-225 9000.

CAR PARKS

At the east end of Princes Street, at the top of Leith Street, are car parks at Greenside (tel: 0131-558 3518) and the St James Centre (National Car Parks Ltd), tel: 0131-556 5066. The Waverley Car Park is located at 6 New Street, behind Waverley Station (tel: 0131-557 8526), and NCP also operate a car park at Castle Terrace, off Lothian Road (tel: 0131-229 2870).

Facts for the Visitor

TOURIST INFORMATION

The Edinburgh and Scotland Tourist

Waverley, Edinburgh's main station

Information Centre is located on top of Princes Mall at the east end of Princes Street. Open Mon–Sat 9am–6pm, Sun 10am–6pm, closes 5pm Nov–Mar, Sun–Wed; later closing at 7pm daily in May, June and Sept and 8pm daily Jul–Aug. The staff can assist with accommodation, bookings, advance reservations and ticket sales, and there is a shop selling souvenirs, maps and guidebooks, a bureau de change and an on-line information facility. Tel: 0845-225 5121; www.edinburgh.org

There is also a branch of this information desk at Edinburgh Airport (Apr–Oct: daily 6.30am–10.30pm; Nov–Mar: daily 7.30am–9.30pm).

TRAVEL SERVICES

American Express, 69 George Street: tel: 0131-718 2505; foreign exchange, tel: 0131-718 2501.
Thomas Cook, 26–28 Frederick Street, tel: 0131-465 7700.

CASH DISPENSERS AND LINK MACHINES

Abbey: Hanover Street
Barclays: St Andrew Square
Clydesdale: Hanover Street and other branches
HBOS: The Mound and other branches
HSBC: Hanover Street
Lloyds TSB: Hanover Street and other branches
National Westminster: George Street
Nationwide: George Street
Royal Bank of Scotland: St Andrew Square and other branches

Open-top bus tours
Several bus companies run sightseeing city tours on open-top double-decker buses. All have frequent departures from Waverley Bridge. Details for all companies can be obtained at: 0131-555 6363.

CURRENCY

The monetary unit is the pound sterling, as in the rest of Great Britain: £1 = 100 pence. In addition to the Bank of England notes and coins, notes issued by the Bank of Scotland and Royal Bank of Scotland are also in circulation (same value and size, different designs).

Bank notes come in denominations of £1, £5, £10, £20, £50 and £100, and there are 1, 2, 5, 10, 20, 50 pence and £1 and £2 coins. Scottish bank notes are legal tender throughout Britain, but you may have difficulty changing them elsewhere.

POSTAL SERVICES

The main post office customer service is in the St James Centre at the east end of Princes Street, tel: 0845-722 3344. Other city centre post offices are at 40 Frederick Street and 33 Forrest Street (near the University).

INTERNET SERVICES

Easyeverything, 58 Rose Street, tel: 0131-220 3577.
Internet Café, 98 West Bow, tel: 0131-226 5400.

NEWSPAPERS

The Scotsman and *Scotland on Sunday* have detailed reports on Scottish affairs, as well as international news – the latter also has good restaurant tips and travel and culture articles. Foreign visitors will find a comprehensive range of overseas newspapers and periodicals available at International Newsagents, 351 High Street, tel 0131-225 4827. Other Scottish and English daily papers are widely available.

EMERGENCIES

Police, ambulance, fire brigade: **999** (for emergencies only).
Lothian & Borders Police Headquar-

ters, Fettes Avenue, tel: 0131-311 3131.

Royal Infirmary of Edinburgh, tel: 0131-536 1000.

Western General Hospital, tel: 0131-537 1000.

LOST AND FOUND

Lost items are invariably handed in to police stations and passed to the Police Headquarters, Fettes Avenue, Edinburgh EH4 1RB, tel: 0131-311 3141. For belongings mislaid on public transport, the appropriate company should be contacted.

Waverley Railway Station, tel: 0845-711 4141.

Lothian Buses, tel: 0131-554 4494.

DISABLED ACCESS

For a largely Georgian/Victorian city, Edinburgh is remarkably well equipped for those with disabilities, although public transport can be a problem. Many taxis carry a wheelchair symbol on the front. With a few exceptions, most public buildings now have wheelchair facilities and there are rigid conditions for new building.

For advice, contact Capability Scotland, tel: 0131-313 5510. For venue and transport access in the city, contact Grapevine, tel: 0131-475 2370, or Lothian Shopmobility, tel: 0131-225 9559.

PHOTOGRAPHY

In the majority of Edinburgh's museums, castles and art galleries, photography is not allowed. In some cases permission can be obtained, but flash photography is not encouraged.

PUBLIC HOLIDAYS

New Year's Day, 2 January, Good Friday, the first Monday in May, the last Monday in May, the first Monday in August and 25 and 26 December.

Tipping
Most restaurants do not add a service charge to the bill. In this case it is usual, but not compulsory, to give a 10–15 percent tip. If a service charge has been included in the bill, you will not be expected to pay extra unless you wish to reward exceptional service. A similar percentage tip should be paid to hairdressers and taxi drivers. A tip of at least £1 is appropriate for porters. It is not necessary to tip in self-service establishments or pubs.

WALKING TOURS

Entertaining guided walking tours of the Old Town, mostly in the evenings with a ghost theme, include: Mercat Tours (also daytime history tours, tel: 0131-557 6464), featuring storytelling in atmospheric closes and underground vaults; Auld Reekie Tours (tel: 0131-557 4700) with 'jumper-ooters'.

SPECTATOR SPORTS
Rugby

Internationals are held between January and March at Murrayfield Stadium on Corstorphine Road under the auspices of the Scottish Rugby Union, tel: 0131-346 5000.

Football

Edinburgh has two Premier League clubs, Heart of Midlothian and Hibernian. Heart of Midlothian (tel: 0131-200 7200; www.heartsfc.co.uk) have their ground at Tynecastle, on Gorgie Road, at the west end of the city, and Hibernian (tel: 0131-661 1875; www.hibs.co.uk) play at Easter Road, north of London Road, at the east end. There are matches usually on Saturdays and Wednesdays throughout the season.

Horse Racing

Twenty-two race meetings, Flat and National Hunt, are held every year at

Musselburgh Racecourse, tel: 0131-665 2859. Meetings are usually held mid-week.

Edinburgh for Children

During the summer, **Portobello Beach** makes for a diverting seaside excursion for children *(see page 77)*, although its glamour has long faded for adults.

Edinburgh Zoo *(see page 83)* and **Deep Sea World** (tel: 01383 411 880), over the Forth Road Bridge at North Queensferry, are recommended diversions. The aquarium gives a diver's eye-view of the denizens of the deep. For the more active child, the water-slides at **Leith Waterworld** (tel: 0131-555 6000) are a real treat. Most of the sports centres *(see page 110)* offer soft play (bouncy castles etc.), gymnastics and trampolining.

The **Camera Obscura and World of Illuminations** at Outlook Tower, Castle Hill *(see page 23)*, is popular with children, but **Our Dynamic Earth**, at the other end of the Royal Mile *(see page 37)* will keep them enthralled for longer. One of Scotland's biggest Millennium projects,

In the foyer of Our Dynamic Earth

Our Dynamic Earth, housed in a futuristic building, tells the story of the planet through state of the art earthscapes, with plenty of interactive elements.

Our Dynamic Earth is good for learning, as is **Shaping a Nation** at Fountainpark (tel: 0131-229 0300), which uses similar technology to explore the achievements of famous Scots. Boisterous children who enjoy a bit of blood and gore will love the Edinburgh Dungeon *(see box on page 32)*, but it's not suitable for timid younger ones.

There are plenty of fun walks around the city; older and more energetic kids will enjoy scrambling up Arthur's Seat *(see page 36)* or Calton Hill *(see page 44)*.

During the **Edinburgh Festival** the streets are full of jugglers and performance artists, and on Fringe Sunday in The Meadows there are side-shows and numerous distractions, such as face-painting workshops. But be warned that the crowds can become exhausting.

The **Edinburgh International Science Festival** in April (tel: 0131-558 7666) features children's events, and in May/June Edinburgh hosts the **Children's International Theatre Festival** (tel: 0131-225 8050).

ACCOMMODATION

Accommodation ranges from luxury hotels to backpackers' hostels, and the listings below include options to suit all pockets. B&B in a guest house or private home can be good value, from £15 per person sharing. The Scottish Tourist Board star gradings range from 1 star (fair and acceptable) to 5 stars (exceptional/world class).

Except for 5-star hotels, most prices quoted include cooked Scottish breakfast. Approximate prices per person per night in a hotel double room are: **££££** = over £75; **£££** = £50–75; **££** = £30–50; **£** = below £30.

For guest houses, private hotels and B&B establishments: **££** = £25–40; **£** = £15–25.

Prices may be higher during August while out-of-season prices are frequently lower.

City Centre Hotels

££££

Albany Hotel, 39–43 Albany Street, tel: 0131-556 0397, www.albanyhotel edinburgh.co.uk A luxury listed Georgian hotel on a quiet New Town street.

Apex International Hotel, 31–35 Grassmarket, tel: 0131-300 3456, www.apexhotels.co.uk In the centre of the Old Town, with views of the castle; rooftop restaurant and onsite parking.

Balmoral Hotel, 1 Princes Street, tel: 0131-556 2414, www.thebalmoralhotel.com Imposing five-star hotel at the east end of Edinburgh's main shopping street. Excellent service and every luxury.

The Bonham, 35 Drumsheugh Gardens, tel: 0131-226 6050, www.thebonham.com Victorian hotel with stylish contemporary décor in the smart West End.

Caledonian Hilton, Princes Street, tel: 0131-222 8888, www.hilton.com Esteemed five-star hotel at the west end of Princes Street, with top-notch facilities.

Channings, 15 South Learmonth Gardens, tel: 0131-315 2226, www.channings.co.uk Comfortable, tastefully decorated Edwardian town house hotel on a quiet street off Queensferry Road.

George Hotel, 19–21 George Street, tel: 0131-225 1251, www.principal-hotels.com Distinguished hotel well situated in the heart of the New Town.

The Howard Hotel, 32–36 Great King Street, tel: 0131-557 3500, www.thehoward.com Quiet, luxuriously decorated hotel in the New Town. First-class basement restaurant.

Radisson SAS Hotel, 80 High Street, tel: 0131-557 9797, www.edinburgh.radissonsas.com Despite the appearance of vernacular architecture, this is a modern luxury hotel on the historic Royal Mile. Use of pool and gym.

Royal Terrace Hotel, 18 Royal Terrace, tel: 0131-557 3222, www.theroyal terracehotel.co.uk Handsome chintzy hotel in the New Town.

Sheraton Grand Hotel & Spa, 1 Festival Square, tel: 0131-229 9131, www.sheraton.com/grandedinburgh Five-star hotel in the heart of Edinburgh's financial and theatre district.

£££

The Carlton Hotel, North Bridge, tel: 0131-472 3000, www.paramount-hotels.co.uk Good location at Edinburgh's east end, a short step from the Royal Mile

Book ahead
Advance booking is essential throughout the summer months, and particularly during August when the city can be filled to capacity and visitors have to be diverted to Stirling, Perth or Glasgow. The Edinburgh and Scotland Tourist Information Centre provides a room-finding service, tel: 0131-473 3800.

and Princes Street. Four stars, with a top-class leisure centre and excellent facilities.

Menzies Belford Hotel, 69 Belford Road, tel: 0131-332 2545, www.menzieshotels.co.uk By the Water of Leith, within walking distance of the city centre.

Mount Royal Hotel, 53 Princes Street, tel: 0131-225 7161, www.ramadajarvis.co.uk Ramada Jarvis hotel in a prime location in the city's main shopping street, with views of the castle.

Point Hotel, 34 Bread Street, tel: 0131-221 5555, www.point-hotel.co.uk Refurbished in contemporary style. Close to theatre and financial centre.

££

Jurys Edinburgh Inn, 43 Jeffrey Street, tel: 0131-200 3300, www.jurysinns.com City centre hotel just a few minutes walk from Waverley Station and all attractions, ideal for business or leisure.

The Lodge Hotel, 6 Hampton Terrace, West Coates, tel: 0131-337 3682, www.thelodgehotel.co.uk Small, elegant and family-run, close to Haymarket Station and the International Conference Centre.

Thrums Private Hotel, 14–15 Minto Street, tel: 0131-667 5545, www.thrumshoteledinburgh.com Detached Georgian house with garden. Private parking.

£

Travelodge Central, 33 St Mary's Street, tel: 0870-085 0950, fax: 0131-557 3681, www.travelodge.co.uk Budget option in the city centre. Breakfast not included.

GUEST HOUSES
££

Ivy Guest House, 7 Mayfield Gardens, tel: 0131-667 3411, www.ivyguesthouse.com Family run; three-star Victorian house. Eight rooms (six en suite).

City Suburbs & Outskirts
££££

Marriott Dalmahoy Hotel and Country Club, Kirknewton, tel: 0131-333 1845, fax: 0131-333 1433, www.marriott.com A luxurious country mansion 7 miles (11 km) from the city centre, convenient for the airport.

Prestonfield House Hotel, Priestfield Road, tel: 0131-225 7800, www.prestonfield.com Old-world charm with five bedrooms (and 26 in a modern extension) in a 17th-century mansion located under Salisbury Crags. Country setting 10 minutes from the city centre.

£££

Braid Hills Hotel, 134 Braid Road, tel: 0131-447 8888, www.braidhillshotel.co.uk Quiet, Gothic mansion with superb views, only 2½ miles (4 km) from the city centre.

The Edinburgh Marriott, 111 Glasgow Road, tel: 0870-400 7293, www.marriotthotels.com/edieb Modern hotel on the western approach into the city, near the zoo and airport.

Holiday Inn Edinburgh, 132 Corstorphine Road, tel: 0870-400 9026, www.holidayinn.com Modern hotel adjacent to the zoo. Leisure facilities include gym, swimming pool and sauna.

Malmaison Hotel, Tower Place, Leith, tel: 0131-468 5000, www.malmaison.com Superb renovation of former Seamen's Mission building. Art deco style, four-poster beds and a first-class restaurant.

Norton House Hotel, Ingliston, tel: 0131-333 1275, www.handpicked.co.uk Country house hotel close to Edinburgh airport.

££

A-Haven Town House, 180 Ferry Road, tel: 0131-554 6559, www.

a-haven.co.uk Attractive Victorian hotel, 11 rooms with pleasant personal service, situated near the Botanic Garden.

Express by Holiday Inn, Britannia View, Ocean Drive, Leith, tel: 0131-555 4422, www.hiex-edinburgh.com This is a new and comfortable waterfront hotel that overlooks the Ocean Terminal close to the Britannia. The decent room come with all modern conveniences.

GUEST HOUSES
££

Ashlyn Guest House, 42 Inverleith Row, tel: 0131-552 2954, www.ashlyn-edinburgh.com Elegant Georgian house beside the Botanic Garden, tastefully furnished. Seven rooms.

Salisbury Guest House, 45 Salisbury Road, tel: 0131-667 1264, www.salisbury-guest-house.co.uk This is a lovely listed building with comfortable non-smoking accommodation in a good location on the South Side of the city. Eight rooms.

£

Balquhidder Guest House, 94 Pilrig Street, tel: 0131-554 3377, www.olstravel.com/guest/balquid Conservation-listed Victorian former church manse offers a warm family welcome. Six rooms (five en suite).

Galloway Guest House, 22 Dean Park Crescent, 0131-332 3672, e-mail: galloway-theclarks@hotelmail.com A beautifully restored Victorian house situated in the gracious environs of Stockbridge, within easy walking distance of the city centre. Ten rooms (six en suite).

HOSTELS

Edinburgh is a backpacker's paradise; there is a big choice of independent hostels in the heart of the city. There are also two official youth hostels with good facilities run by the **Scottish Youth Hostels Association** (www.syha.org.uk). Prices range from £8.50–17 for a dormitory bed, or £11–25 per person for double occupancy where available. There is no upper age limit for guests.

Backpackers Hostel, 65 Cockburn Street, tel: 0131-220 1717, www.hoppo.com Double and twin rooms and dormitories. Open 24 hours. Very central.

Bruntsfield Youth Hostel, 7 Bruntsfield Crescent, tel: 0870-004 1114, www.syha.org.uk. Dormitories in a leafy area, not quite central. Run by the SYHA.

Eglinton Youth Hostel, 18 Eglinton Crescent, tel: 0870-004 1116, www.syha.org.uk. Dormitories in the West End, run by the SYHA. A magnificent piece of architecture and friendly to boot.

High Street Hostel, 8 Blackfriars Steet, tel: 0131-557 3984, www.scotlands-top-hostels.com Dormitories. Friendly, atmospheric lodging in a 16th-century building in the Old Town. The hostel also runs MacBackpackers – which are fun guided tours of the Scottish Highlands.

Campus rooms

Reasonably priced seasonal accommodation is available in the halls and self-catering flats of the universities. The University of Edinburgh's Pollock Halls, on the edge of Holyrood Park, offer hotel standards and a range of facilities, March to April and June to September, **££**; tel: 0800-028 7118, e-mail: edinburgh.first@ed.ac.uk Cheaper rooms are at the Heriot-Watt campus on the western fringe of the city, year-round, **£**; tel: 0131-451 3669, e-mail: info@eccscotland.com In the summer, May to August, try also Queen Margaret University College, near the zoo, **£**; tel: 0131-317 3314, e-mail: ataylor@qmuc.ac.uk

INDEX